Thomas Haweis

A Familiar and Practical Improvement of the Church Catechism

Designed to Render the Work of Catechising More Easy and Profitable

Thomas Haweis

A Familiar and Practical Improvement of the Church Catechism
Designed to Render the Work of Catechising More Easy and Profitable

ISBN/EAN: 9783743687295

Printed in Europe, USA, Canada, Australia, Japan

Cover: Foto ©Lupo / pixelio.de

More available books at www.hansebooks.com

A
Familiar and Practical Improvement
OF THE
CHURCH CATECHISM:

DESIGNED TO RENDER

The Work of Catechising more Easy and Profitable;

AND THEREBY AFFORD ASSISTANCE TO

MINISTERS, SCHOOLMASTERS, PARENTS,

And whoever may be entrusted with

The Care and Instruction of the RISING GENERATION.

By the Rev. T. HAWEIS, LL.B.

Rector of ALDWINCKLE ALL SAINTS, *Northamptonshire*;
AND CHAPLAIN TO
The Right Honourable the EARL of PETERBOROW.

LONDON:

Printed for EDWARD and CHARLES DILLY, in the Poultry.

M.DCC.LXXV.

PREFACE.

TO ALL
MINISTERS OF THE GOSPEL,
SCHOOLMASTERS, PARENTS,
AND
Whoever are entrusted with the Care of the
RISING GENERATION.

My Brethren,

FOR your assistance in the important work committed to your trust, the following little treatise goes forth into the world. The over-flowings

ings of infidelity and ungodliness are seen on every side. Nor can it well be otherwise, whilst so little attention is paid to the minds of children to inculcate those principles of gospel truth, which alone can enable them, through faith, to resist the allurements of an ensnaring world, and the seductions of a corrupted heart. Shameful ignorance of the first principles of the doctrines of Christ is evident, and whilst the many satisfy themselves with the profession of Christianity, how few are able to give a scriptural reason of the hope which is in them, much less to silence gainsayers with the words of sound doctrine.

The

The obvious usefulness of catechetical instruction, hath produced many helps of this sort. The present proceeds on a method, which, though it seems not hitherto much adopted, carries evident propriety along with it. Tender minds cannot be supposed to be acquainted with the long answers to questions often put in their mouths, which also burdening their memory gives them an aversion to instruction: here the teacher is directed to explain himself so as to be clearly understood, and to engage, if possible, the attention of his pupils, that they may, receiving instruction at his lips, answer intelligibly, not merely repeat by rote, but give some evidence that

that they underſtand what they are taught.

Recommended by near twenty years experience of its uſefulneſs, the method here propoſed is ſubmitted to the conſideration of thoſe who wiſh to be profitable in their generation. And may the gracious Shepherd who enjoined us to feed his lambs, accompany it with his divine benediction!

ALDWINCKLE,
April 25, 1775.

A Familiar

A Familiar and Practical Improvement

OF THE

CHURCH CATECHISM.

Q. WHAT is your name?
A. A——

Q. What do you call this name?
A. My Christian name.

Q. Why do you call it your Christian name?
A. Because it was given me, when at my baptism, I made profession of being a Christian.

Q. But it is not a *name* merely that makes you a Christian, is it?
A. No. I must have the spirit and temper of a Christian, or the name will profit me nothing. Rev. iii. 1. Gal. iii. 27.

Q. Who gave you that name?
A. My godfathers and godmothers.

Q. Why do you call them godfathers and godmothers?
A. Because

A. Becaufe they undertook, as my fpiritual parents, to teach me the things belonging to God and godlinefs.

Q. Is it not a very wicked thing to undertake fuch a charge, and never attempt the performing it?

A. Yes, very wicked.

Q. But don't you think that this is too often the cafe?

A. Yes, I am afraid it is.

C. Indeed my dear child you fay true; godfathers and godmothers often ftand to oblige their friends and relations, and when they have paid their fees, or partaken of the entertainment, and that oftentimes alfo accompanied with intemperance, and lewd converfation, they never trouble their heads about the folemn vow and profeffion they have made.

Q. Will they not in the day of judgment, think you, have a dreadful account to make of fuch rafh engagements, and grievous neglect of the children's fouls?

A. No doubt they will. Their god-childrens fouls if loft by fuch neglect, will be required at their hands.

C. I hope that I your minifter, and your parents, fhall endeavour if you have been thus neglected, to give the greater diligence that you may not continue

tinue in ignorance of your sacramental engagements?

Q. What was the outward form of your baptism?

A. Water was sprinkled upon me in the name of the Father, Son and Holy Ghost.

Q. What was the thing signified by that sprinkling of Water?

A. The sprinkling of the blood of Christ upon my conscience: 1 Pet. iii. 21. Heb. ix. 14.

Q. You wash persons, when they are dirty and filthy, don't you?

A. Yes.

Q. Was the water of baptism designed to represent any such washing?

A. It was. Heb x. 22. Tit. iii. 5. Ephes. v. 26. John iii. 5.

Q. Why? were you, even when born, filthy?

A. Yes.

Q. How came that to be so?

A. Because I was conceived in wickedness, and born in sin. Psal. li. 5.

Q. What? when you came into the world was you wicked, and defiled with sin?

A. Yes, I was a corrupted creature from the womb. Rom. v. 12.

Q. If you were thus born wicked, and a sinner, you deserved to perish, did not you?

A. Yes.

A. Yes. I was by nature a child of wrath. Ephef. ii. 3.

Q. Would God have been juſt in condemning you for the ſin in which you were born?

A. Aſſuredly. Compare Rom. v. 14. with Gen. xviii. 25. Rom. iii. 5, 6.

Q. What is the wages of ſin?

A. Death. Rom. vi. 23.

Q. What death?

A. Death temporal and eternal. Luke xii. 5.

Q. And does every babe that is born in ſin deſerve eternal death?

A. Yes. So God's word ſays.

Q. Many people call children little innocents, don't they?

A. Yes.

Q. But are they innocent?

A. No.

Q. And if they were innocent would they ever die?

A. No, for death is only the wages of ſin.

Q. Are the ſeeds of all ſin ſown in the nature of man before he is born?

A. Yes. Job xiv. 4. Pſal. li. 5.

Q. Is all the wickedneſs therefore in the world the conſequence of our being corrupted creatures by nature?

A. So the ſcripture ſays. Pſal. lviii. 3, 4.

Q. It

Q. It is very desirable to be delivered from the wrath you speak of, is it not?

A. Oh yes, very desirable.

Q. What would become of you if you were not delivered from it?

A. Body and soul would be cast into hell. Psal. ix. 17.

Q. What can only deliver you from sin, and its wages, death and hell?

A. The blood of Christ.

Q. What doth that for you?

A. It cleanseth from all sin. 1 John i. 7.

Q. Who is this Christ you speak of?

A. He is God the Son. John i. 1. Mark i. 11.

Q. What did he for you?

A. He undertook to pay to God the Father a *ransom* for our *sins.* Heb. x. 9. Matt. xx. 28.

Q. How did he accomplish this?

A. He became a little child, took our nature, in it fulfilled the law of God, and died upon a cross.

Q. What benefit could this obtain for you? Did God accept his Son's sacrifice for your sins?

A. Yes, he died the just for the unjust. 1 Pet. iii. 18. Rom. v. 19. Heb. 9. 12.—x. 14.

Q. Do you suppose that the baptism of your body in water represents the washing of your soul in the blood of Christ?

A. I

A. I do. 1 Cor. vi. 11. Heb. ix. 14.

Q. It is not therefore the act of the minister, in sprinkling you, nor the water which washes you that makes you a Christian *indeed?*

A. No. This is but an outward sign of the inward and spiritual grace.

Q. You don't suppose that all whose names are in a parish register, are therefore *real* Christians?

A. No.

C. You are right my dear, only those are true Christians who have the washing of regeneration, and the renewing of the Holy Ghost. Baptism is a figure, and without the thing signified by the sign, it can profit us nothing.—All are admitted to the outward sign who are presented by the communicants as their sponsors.—In the judgment of charity we receive such into the pale of outward profession, presuming they will be brought up in the nurture and admonition of the Lord. Time must prove whether they are *really* of the number of God's faithful and elect children. I hope you my dear little ones will be of that happy number, and be found experiencing what you learn to repeat that the Holy Ghost sanctifieth you with all the elect people of God.

Q. Were you in your baptism admitted to any great blessings and privileges?

A. Yes.

Q. What

Q. What were they?

A. I was made a member of Chrift, a child of God, and an inheritor of the kingdom of heaven.

Q. What do you mean by being made a member of Chrift, a child of God, and an inheritor of the kingdom of heaven? No outward form can effect this, can it?

A. No. Gal iii. 26.

Q. Do you mean then, that the facramental fign and feal of baptifm, gave you a right to claim by faith under the covenant of promife, thefe great and diftinguifhed mercies?

A. I do. Rom. iv. 11.

Q. If you live and die in unbelief, impenitence, and wickednefs, you cannot be a child of God, can you?

A. No, affuredly. Gal. iii. 27.—v. 24.

C. Mind this my dear children, if you grow up to tell lies—to be froward—to quarrel one with another—to hate your bibles—to neglect to pray to God to give you his grace—and be like the many wicked examples around you, inftead of being members of Chrift, children of God, and inheritors of the kingdom of heaven, you will be found members of the wicked one, children of the devil, and inherit wrath to the uttermoft. I pray the Lord Jefus Chrift, that your lot and portion may be with his chosen ones, who being baptized into Christ have put on Christ.

II.

C. You told me, when you were baptized, that you were admitted to claim some great and distinguished privileges, what is the first of them?

A. To become a member of Christ.

Q. What? A member of Christ's body as your hand and foot are members of your own body?

A. Yes. 1 Cor vi. 15.—xii. 12. Eph. v. 30.

Q. Christ hath a natural human body, like yours, hath he not?

A. Yes.

Q. Hath he also a mystical body composed of all faithful people, of whom he is the head?

A. Yes. Eph. v. 23.—i. 22.—iv. 15. Col. i. 18.

Q. Of which of these are you a member, of his natural or mystical body?

A. Of Christ's mystical body.

Q. Is this any blessing, or advantage to you?

A. Yes, inexpressibly great.

Q. What were you before you were a member of Christ?

A. Dead in trespasses and sins. Eph. ii. 1, 2, 3.

Q. How came you then to be alive unto God? Are you grafted into Christ?

A. Yes,

A. Yes. Eph. ii. 4, 5.

C. But for this you must have been as a dry branch, cut off and withered fit fuel only for the fire, John xv. 6.

Q. If you are a member of Christ, doth he love you as his own flesh and blood; feel for you; guard you; and will he never leave and forsake you?

A. So, I believe and hope.

Q. Is it not then highly your duty, and should it not be your delight to love Christ your head, and his people your fellow members?

A. Yes assuredly. 1 John iv. 13, 21.

Q. It is by such a Christian spirit that you must prove you belong to Christ?

A. Certainly. John xiii. 35.

Q. What is the second distinguished privilege to which you are admitted in baptism?

A. To become a child of God.

Q. Why? Were you not born a child of God?

A. No. I was his creature, but not his child.

Q. How came this about?

A. By Adam's sin. Rom. v. 12.

Q. Who was he?

A. The first man.

Q. Was he the child of God? Did God create him in his own image and likeness?

A. Yes. Gen. i. 27.

Q. How came he to forfeit his mercies?

A. He sinned.

Q. Where?

A. In Paradise.

Q. And did he lose God's image and likeness, by his fall into sin?

A. He did. 1 John iii. 8.

Q. Did all his posterity suffer for his fall?

A. Yes, they fell in him. Rom. v. 12, 17, 19.

Q. Are none of the children of Adam now born children of God?

A. None.

Q. Are they born in the likeness of Adam, when bearing God's image, or when he had lost it by his fall?

A. When he had lost it. Gen. v. 3.

Q. Then you are a child of Adam by nature, are you?

A. I am.

Q. How come you then to say you are a child of God? Has God taken back any of Adam's posterity into this blessed relation again?

A. Yes, many.

Q. How is this done?

A. By adoption, and grace.

Q. Do you mean by this, that God in his Son Christ Jesus, and for his sake is pleased graciously to pardon, and readmit into his family some of the fallen children of Adam?

A.

A. I do. Eph. i. 4—7.

Q. And do you suppose that baptism is appointed as the sign of your readmission into God's family?

A. Yes. Matt. xxviii. 19.

Q. Is it a great favour and blessing to have God for your father?

A. The greatest in the world.

Q. If you are God's child, you expect that God will love you—provide for you—watch over you—and lead you in his holy ways.

A. I trust he will.

Q. What is your duty then if God is so good to you, as to make you his child? Should you love him as a father [a]—fear him [b]—depend upon his care [c]—pray to him [d]—submit to his providences [e]—and be patient under his corrections?

A. Yes, no doubt I ought.

C. I pray God for you, my dear children, that you may remember this. All that the tenderest father ever shewed you of affection and kindness is infinitely short of what your father in heaven hath done and is doing for his children; and if there cannot be a more shocking character, than an unnatural, undutiful and disobedient child to an earthly parent: how much more wicked and ungrateful would you be, if you professed yourselves

---

[a] Prov. xxiii. 26.
[b] Psal. cxii. 1.
[c] 1 Pet. v. 7. Matt. vi. 25.
[d] Eph. vi. 18. Luke xviii. 1.
[e] Heb. xii. 9.

to be children of God, and yet lived and died as the children of the wicked one?

Q. What is the third privilege to which you were admitted at your baptifm?

A. To be an inheritor of the kingdom of heaven.

Q. You have heard then, I fuppofe, that there is a heaven and a hell, do you believe it?

A. Yes, I do.

Q. Which of thefe do you expect to go to when you are dead?

A. To heaven, I hope.

Q. I pray the Lord of life and glory, to bring you there, my dear child! But do not all in general hope to go to heaven when they die?

A. They do.

Q. But will every perfon go to heaven?

A. No, not every one.

Q. Will not fome, yea many, very many, go into hell when they die, think you?

A. I am perfuaded they will. Matt. vii. 13, 14.

C. Yes, my dear children, all the wicked who die in their fins, will be caft into hell; and broad is the gate, and wide the way that leadeth to deftruction, and many there be that go in thereat; for ftrait is the gate, and narrow the way which leadeth unto life, and few there be that find it. This is an awful and alarming truth, which the many cannot be perfuaded to receive, becaufe they

are

are not of that few. I hope you will be found of the bleſſed number, who ſhall enter into the joy of their Lord. You ſay you hope ſo. Who are thoſe therefore who ſhall inherit the kingdom of heaven?

A. They that are members of Chriſt and children of God upon earth. Rom. viii. 17.

Q. You don't think any others can be ſaved?

A. No.

Q. Either of you, I dare ſay, would think it a great thing if you were heir to the richeſt man in the pariſh, and to inherit all his wealth and ſubſtance, would not you?

A. Yes.

C. Ah, my dears, if you were children of princes, and could inherit crowns and kingdoms, they would appear but poor things when you conſider yourſelves as dying worms, in a dying world, what can we carry into the grave with us of theſe things? Nothing. Naked came we into the world, and in the ſame condition muſt the greateſt prince, as well as the meaneſt beggar, go out of it, and carry with him none of his pomp when he dieth. The only ſubſtantial and truly deſireable portion under the ſun is that which the children of God enjoy. They are heirs of God, and joint heirs with Chriſt. If this be your ſtate, if you had not bread to eat, or rags to cover your nakedneſs, you would be richer than the wealth of worlds could make you,

and

and more honourable in the sight of God, the fountain of true honour, than the kings of the earth. I cannot make you heirs to a great estate, or ennoble you; but, my dear children, I can tell you how you may become children of God, and inheritors of his kingdom, which is far better. Don't you think so?

A. I do.

C. I hope you do. I am sure you will when you come to die.

III.

C. You have been telling me of the distinguished privileges into which you were admitted at your baptism. And I wish you deeply and seriously to remember them. I think the least boy or girl of you all is old enough to know how desireable it is to have God for your father, and heaven for your home. And if so, will be careful to seek in the first place the kingdom of God, which you are called thus to inherit. This you engaged to do, when at your baptism you were numbered among God's professing people, and being of too tender years to speak for yourselves, your godfathers and godmothers solemnly engaged to teach you, as soon as you should be able to learn, what a solemn vow, promise and profession you then made, by them your sureties. Whether they have discharged

their

their duty or not, I know not. Dreadful carelessness in this matter is but too common. But be that as it may, you are now of years to understand what they engaged for on your behalf. And if you would receive any effectual blessing in consequence of your baptism, and actually enjoy the high privilege of being Christians, you must be found walking before God as dear children. As you acknowledge this to be your bounden duty and service, I desire therefore to know, whether you can tell me, what did your godfathers and godmothers in your baptism promise for you?

A. They did promise and vow three things in my name, 1st. That I should renounce the devil and all his works, the pomps and vanities of this wicked world, and all the sinful lusts of the flesh. 2dly. That I should believe all the articles of the Christian faith. And 3dly. That I should keep God's holy word and commandments, and walk in the same all the days of my life.

Q. Well now mind—Three things you say they promised for you. What is the first of them?

A. 1. That I should renounce the devil and all his works, the pomps and vanities of this wicked world, and all the sinful lusts of the flesh.

Q. Very well. So that you see that the first article of your engagement with God, as the grateful return due for his infinite mercy and grace in calling you to his holy baptism, is that you should

should renounce, resist, oppose, and manfully under Christ's banner's fight against a wicked devil, a wicked world, and a wicked heart. This is the Christian's warfare, and under the conduct of the great captain of his salvation he goeth on conquering and to conquer. What is the first enemy of Christ and your soul which you engage to renounce and fight against?

A. The devil and all his works.

Q. You have heard that there is such a being as the devil, the grand enemy of God and man, have you not?

A. Yes.

Q. Do you know what he is in his nature?

A. A wicked and fallen spirit.

C. My dear, you answer right. The devil is a wicked and fallen spirit—he hath not a body as we have, he is a spirit. God created him a glorious archangel: in heaven pride entered into his heart, and he rebelled against God and his anointed. He drew by his wiles multitudes of the angels to join him in his rebellion: for which God in just judgment cast them down from their high estate, and reserves them in chains of darkness, unto the judgment of the great day. These wicked spirits are permitted now to go to and fro in the earth to try the fidelity of the children of God, (carrying always their hell with them) and are maliciously

bent

bent to seduce us from our allegiance, that we may share with them in their guilt and punishment. Therefore we are called upon to resist the devil, that he may flee from us, that is, to reject his temptations and allurements to sin.

Many foolish persons frighten little children with terrible stories of the devil, and his coming to them, and as foolish and absurd pictures even in our prayer-books represent the devil as black, with horns and hoofs, and a tail, as if he were some strange beast. But, my dears, all this is ridiculous, false and absurd. He is a spirit, and hath no body, nor parts of a body. Never did he appear in any such shape or form, 'tis a bug-bear; you never need be afraid of such a phantom. No. If ever he appeared, he would not come in a figure to be loathed, but to be loved; and therefore St. Paul saith he transforms himself into an angel of light. If the devil appeared as he is, and we could see his real character and designs he would be abhorred, and detested. But the way he works is as a spirit having access to our spirits, presenting to our senses such outward objects as would allure us to sin, and suggesting to us that evil, which would make us in our souls like himself.

Q. Are there many devils?

A. Yes, great multitudes. Mark v. 9.

Q. Is there a prince of the devils?

A. Is

A. Yes.

Q. Is his name particularly mentioned in fcripture?

A. Yes. He is called by many names, Satan, Beelzebub, Apollyon, Abaddon.

Q. What is his *work?*

A. To fin himfelf, and tempt others to commit fin. 1 John iii. 8.

Q. May the children of the devil then be known in this world?

A. Yes.

Q. How are they to be known?

A. By their works. Matt. vii. 20.

Q. Are lyars the children of the devil?

A. Yes. John viii. 44.

C. Mind now what you are faying, or you will be condemned out of your own mouth. The devil was a lyar from the beginning. Take care to fpeak the truth always if you would be God's children, and not have the devil for your father.

Q. Is fighting and quarreling and murder the work of the devil?

A. Yes. He was a murderer from the beginning.

C. Take notice of this, and be always kind and loving one to another, and never quarrel, and fight and fcratch, and abufe one another.

Q. Are

Q. Are disobedient children the children of the wicked one?

A. Yes. He is the spirit that worketh in the children of disobedience.

C. Well then, be sure be dutiful and obedient to your parents, do as they bid you, without murmuring, and be more afraid of all sin and wickedness, because it makes you like the devil, than because you will be beaten if you are caught doing what is evil.—Your first grand enemy is the devil, him you profess to renounce and all his works. What is the second enemy of your soul that you renounce?

A. The pomps and vanities of this wicked world.

Q. Is this a good or a wicked world?

A. A wicked world.

Q. But remember, the things of the world in themselves are not evil; for every creature of God is good, but the devil's children, who abuse the good creatures of God, make the wickedness of the world. Are the generality of mankind good or evil?

A. Very evil. The whole world lieth in wickedness.

Q. What do you renounce in this wicked world?

A. The pomps and vanities of it.

C. The

C. The pomp, pride, and vanities of the world are the things which the devil employs to seduce and enslave mens hearts, and by these he maintains his kingdom in the world. Hence he is called the god of this world. The world and the things of it in themselves, as God's creatures, are all good, but perverted by our corruption they become occasions of evil: the wealth and honours of it minister to mens pride and covetousness. They love mammon more than God, and prefer gold to godliness, and the honour which cometh from man, to that which cometh from God only; worshipping and serving the creature more than the Creator. Such pomps and vanities pursued make the world to be called this wicked world.

Q. Are the pomps and vanities of the world confined only to the rich and great?

A. No.

Q. Are poor persons, such as you, children, or your parents, in danger from the pomps and vanities of this wicked world?

A. Yes, as well as others.

C. True, my dear, pride and covetousness are bound up in the heart of every man, and the things of the world draw these forth into act, in whatever station we are placed, if the grace of God does not restrain the evil. A poor man may be as proud in a cottage, as the rich in a palace.—A little girl,

like

like you, may be as proud of a fine ribband or a new gown, as the lady who is decked in brocade and diamonds. A labourer, who has learned to read and write may be as vain of his scholarship among his equals, as the most puffed up worldly wiseman, who looks down upon him with contempt, and the same coveting of the wealth of the world—pride in what they possess—and discontent in what they want or are disappointed of, appears equally in the lowest as well as highest stations of life.

Q. What further do you profess to renounce?
A. All the sinful lusts of the flesh.
Q. Why, are there any lusts of the flesh that are not sinful?
A. Yes.
C. True. For we must distinguish between desires of the flesh that are natural, and agreeable to God's order, and those which are otherwise. Moderate rest, convenient food and raiment, and bodily exercise, may be profitably as well as pleasingly made use of; and marriage, we know is honourable among all, and the bed undefiled. These are desires of the flesh, and only become sinful by intemperate indulgence. Can you tell me then what lusts of the flesh as sinful you have engaged to renounce?
A. Adultery and fornication.

Q. Are

Q. Are you not also to renounce all lewd desires, lewd looks, and lewd actions, lewd dresses, lewd words, lewd books, or whatever would lead to fornication and uncleanness?

A. Yes, assuredly. Prov. vi. 17. Rom. xiii. 14.

Q. Are these things equally forbidden of God, as the proper deeds of lewdness?

A. Yes. Matt. v. 28.

Q. Is drunkenness, think you, a sinful lust of the flesh?

A. It is.

Q. And gluttony?

A. Yes.

C. They are so. For they inflame the body, and stir up wicked desires. And no man can take fire into his bosom, and not be burnt.

Q. What think you of sloth, is that too a sinful lust of the flesh?

A. Yes.

C. The idle and slothful are ready for the first temptation. When people sleep not for refreshment, but loiter upon their beds to harbour evil thoughts, when bodily ease and pleasure are their chief study,—when they are sauntering away their time with companions as idle as themselves—or by promiscuous intercourse of the sexes in dances, revellings and such like, stir up evil desires, the consequence cannot but follow that sensual appetite

will

will enslave the body, and destroy the soul. Remember therefore, my dear children, and begin early to flee these things.

IV.

C. Your godfathers and godmothers promised three things for you at your baptism, you say, the first of which was, that you should renounce the devil, &c. What is the second thing which they promised for you?

A. That I should believe all the articles of the Christian faith.

Q. Is faith essential to the character of a Christian?

A. Certainly.

Q. Shall every one that believes the articles of the Christian faith be saved?

A. Assuredly. Mark xvi. 16.

Q. What will become of those who believe not?

A. They that believe not shall be damned.

Q. Where are the articles of the Christian faith to be sought and found?

A. In the Bible.

Q. Where are they shortly collected and summed up?

A. In the creeds commonly called the Apostle's,—the Nicene,—and Athanasian.

Q. Are

Q. Are you bound to believe *all* the articles of the Christian faith?

A. Yes, all of them.

Q. Your godfathers and godmothers promised that you should believe all the articles of the Christian faith, did they not?

A. They did.

Q. But faith is the gift of God, is it not?

A. Yes. Eph. ii. 8.

C. You cannot therefore mean that it was in your godfather's or godmother's power to make you believe, what they undertook can only imply, that as soon as you should be able to learn they would instruct you in the principles of the Christian faith, see that you were taught your creed and catechism—set before you the evidence on which your faith stands—call upon you to hear sermons, because faith cometh by hearing, and hearing by the word of God—exhort you to a diligent attendance on all the means of grace, and pray for you that the means may be effectual to your real conversion. More than this they could not engage for.—Whether they have done so or not should be their serious enquiry, or much guilt will lie upon them. With regard to yourselves, however, you will be left without excuse, if now that I am explaining to you these things, you should be inattentive and careless. It is a matter, my my dear children, of infinite importance to you, whether you live and die in faith and in God's favour or out of it. And therefore am I thus employed, that if it please God he would make you to know by my mouth the things that make for your everlasting peace, and give you the true faith of his elect, that you may believe indeed to the saving of your soul.

Q. What is the third thing your godfathers and godmothers promised for you?

A. That I should keep God's holy will and commandments, and walk in the same all the days of my life.

Q. Has true faith always a powerful influence on the practice?

A. Yes.

Q. What doth it produce in the heart?

A. Love to God. Gal. v. 6.

Q. Is there any real love of God but from faith as its root?

A. No. We love him, because we believe he first loved us.

Q. What is the essence of true morality?

A. The love of God in the heart. Rom. xiii. 10.

Q. Can any of God's commandments be in any measure kept, if we are not under the influence of the love of God?

A. No, in no wise.

Q. Are God's will and commandments altogether holy, just and good?

A. Yes. Rom. vii. 12.

Q. Is the *will of his providence* always best, and whatever he ordains, should you submit to it with entire resignation?

A. That is my bounden duty. Psal. xxxix. 9.

Q. Then you are never to murmur under poverty,—under sickness,—under afflictions,—under disappointments, — under oppression?—

A. I ought not.

Q. But it is very trying and difficult to be thus wholly resigned to God's will and pleasure, is it not?

A. Yes. The flesh is ready to complain and rebel.

Q. This then should humble you, should it not, and shew you what a poor sinner you are, and how short you come in keeping God's holy will?

A. Yes, it should.

C. Well, see that it doth then, and lead you every day to the Saviour of sinners, Jesus Christ, for pardon and peace, for he is the advocate for his people when they sin, and pleads his blood as their perpetual propitiation.

Q. You engaged in your baptism to obey God's precepts as well as submit to his providences, did you not?

A. Yes

A. Yes.

Q. Are all God's commandments holy, most meet for him to enjoin, and most fit for you to obey?

A. Certainly.

Q. What is sin?

A. The transgression of God's law.

Q. What is the wages of sin?

A. Death eternal.

Q. What? Doth every transgression of God's commands deserve God's wrath and damnation?

A. Yes, it doth.

Q. That is a very dreadful thing then, is it not?

A. Indeed it is.

Q. Can there be such a thing then as a little sin, against this holy God?

A. No.

Q. Is he that offendeth in one point guilty of all?

A. Yes. James ii. 10.

C. True, for every sin little or great is an open renunciation of the authority of God over us.

Q. Do you think any person keeps the whole law and commandments of God?

A. No. All have sinned. Rom. iii. 23.

Q. Yet you promise to walk in his commandments all the days of your life?

A. I

A. I do.

Q. You own this is your bounden duty then?

A. No doubt it is.

Q. Do you approve of God's law though it condemns you?

A. I do. God is righteous, but I am a sinner.

Q. You cannot therefore bear that God should enter into judgment with you as having kept all his commandments?

A. No. I cannot indeed. In many things we all offend.

Q. Will your own best obedience save you?

A. No, in no wise.

Q. Who then is your salvation?

A. Christ. Acts iv. 12.

Q. Did he fulfil the law of God and all righteousness for you?

A. He did. Rom. x. 4.

Q. Doth he justify you then before God though a poor ungodly sinner?

A. I trust he doth.

Q. But tho' the commandments of God through your weakness and corruption cannot be kept perfectly, and procure you life, as a covenant of works: they are still your rule of duty, are they not?

A. They are.

Q. And as such you take them for your guide, do you not?

A. I

A. I hope to do so.

C. I pray God you may, and every day get a deeper discovery of God's mind and will, and experience a warmer desire to be conformed to it. All God's children are obedient children, and though they place no dependance upon their obedience to justify them before God, in whose sight can no flesh living be justified, yet do they watch and pray that their ways may be made direct before God's face, and that they may be enabled to let their light shine before men, adorning the doctrine of God our Saviour in all things.

V.

C. I have been endeavouring summarily to set before you on the one hand the great and distinguished blessings to which those who are truly baptised into Christ are admitted, and on the other hand the obligations under which such baptised persons lie, of living by faith, renouncing all evil, and walking in God's ways. You, my dear children, were unable, when you were presented at the font, to understand either the privileges or the obligations of your baptism. You were infants—but born of professing parents, to whose children as well as themselves the promises are made—and as capable of admission into the pale of the church of

Christ, as an Israelitish child was by circumcision to be admitted into it, to which rite baptism succeeds—also godly persons, or those, who as partakers of the Lord's table ought to be so, since none should dare to approach the Lord's table unrenewed in the spirit of their minds, such godly persons having undertaken for your early instruction, that you might be brought up in the nurture and admonition of the Lord — On all these accounts you were permitted, though infants, to be initiated under the seal of the covenant, baptised into the number of God's people, and admitted into his church and all the privileges of it; but now that you are grown to some ability of understanding what a solemn vow, promise, and profession they made for you: I as your minister in the face of God and this congregation, do, as is my duty, ask of you, whether you really think you are bound to believe and do as they your godfathers and godmothers promised for you?

A. Yes verily, and by God's help so I will; and I heartily thank our heavenly Father, that he hath called me to this state of salvation, through Jesus Christ our Saviour: and I pray unto God to give me his grace, that I may continue in the same unto my life's end.

C. I am glad to hear you make so full a confession of so gracious a purpose. I pray God for you

you that you may be found faithful. Mind my dear children what you are saying. You are now taking upon yourselves all that your godfathers and godmothers promised in your name, and you will be false to God and your own souls if you draw back from it—will forfeit all the blessings of baptism—and if you should have a lie in your mouth, with the cross of Christ marked on your forehead, you will have the wrath of God upon your souls. Consider then seriously what you are answering. Do you really think you are bound to believe and do as they promised for you? Answer me.

A. Yes, verily.

Q. But you do not undertake this I hope in your own strength?

A. No. Our strength is but weakness.

Q. By what means do you hope to succeed?

A. By God's help, so I will. John xv. 5.

Q. Must God therefore work in you both to *will* and to *do* of his good pleasure?

A. Yes. Salvation is from God alone.

Q. Do you suppose you are now admitted into a state of salvation?

A. I do.

Q. Through whose merits?

A. Through Jesus Christ our Saviour.

Q. Is there no salvation out of Christ?

A. None. Acts iv. 12.

Q. You

Q. You were born a sinner, and as such were in a state of damnation, were you not?

A. I was by nature.

Q. Is Christ come to seek and save that which was lost?

A. Yes.

Q. Is he a Saviour to the uttermost to all that come to God by him?

A. He is.

Q. Can they therefore never perish whom he undertakes to save?

A. No, never. John x. 28.

Q. Is not this matter of inexpressible comfort if we believe it truly?

A. It is.

Q. Ought you not to be exceedingly thankful to God for his unspeakable mercy?

A. I desire to be so, and heartily thank our heavenly Father, who hath called me into this state of salvation through Jesus Christ our Saviour.

Q. Do you suppose, that God for Christ's sake is now become your father?

A. I do.

Q. I hope you will continue in this blessed state and relation unto your life's end, and I dare say you desire so to do.

A. That is indeed my desire.

Q. What

Q. What means do you make use of for this blessed end and purpose?

A. I pray unto God to give me his grace that I may continue in the same (state of salvation to which I am admitted) unto my life's end.

Q. Has God appointed prayer as the means?

A. Yes. He hath. Luke xv. 9—13.

Q. Is he the God that heareth prayer?

A. Yes. He is. John xiv. 13, 14.

Q. And hath he promised to give his Holy Spirit of all grace to them that ask him?

A. He hath. Luke xi. 13.

Q. Then you depend upon God's grace alone to keep you from falling, and not upon your own strength or resolutions?

A. I depend upon his grace alone.

Q. Is God able to keep you in that state of salvation into which he hath called you?

A. Yes, fully able.

Q. But hath he promised to do so whilst you call upon him?

A. Yes, he hath. Psal. l. 15.

Q. Why then you can never perish, but must have everlasting life?

A. That is my confidence.

Q. Shall none be able to pluck you out of his hands?

A. None.

Q. But hath God promifed to pour out a fpirit of prayer and fupplication upon his children?

A. Yes, he hath; becaufe we are fons, he hath fent the Spirit of his Son into our hearts, whereby we cry, Abba Father.

C. Remember this, my dear children, to your great and endlefs comfort, your heavenly Father who brought you into this ftate of falvation, hath ordained the means and the end. The end is falvation. The means of abiding in it is prayer, for which he enables you, and to which he difpofes the hearts of his children, and then the confequence is infallible. I give unto my fheep, fays Chrift, eternal life, and they fhall never perifh, and none fhall pluck them out of my Father's hand. Oh be thankful then for your holy vocation and calling into this ftate of falvation, by Jefus Chrift our Saviour, and give all diligence in God's own appointed means and way, to make your calling and election fure.

VI.

C. Your godfathers and godmothers promifed to inftruct you in the articles of the Chriftian faith, can you repeat your creed.

A. I believe in God the Father Almighty, Maker of heaven and earth: and in Jefus Chrift his only Son our. Lord, who was conceived by the Holy Ghoft, born of the Virgin Mary, fuffered under

under Pontius Pilate, was crucified, dead, and buried; he descended into hell; the third day he rose again from the dead; he ascended into heaven, and sitteth at the right hand of God the Father Almighty, from thence he shall come to judge the quick and the dead. I believe in the Holy Ghost, the holy Catholick church, the communion of saints, the forgiveness of sins, the resurrection of the body, and the life everlasting. Amen.

C. This is your creed then, and it is composed of various articles or joints closely connected with each other. The knowledge of which are of the last importance to your salvation. For this is eternal life to know thee, (says St. John) the only true God and Jesus Christ whom thou hast sent. This knowledge and eternal life are inseparably connected; where God bestows the one we have an infallible certainty that it is the pledge of the other.

Q. How come you by the knowledge of the true God?

A. From the Scriptures.

Q. Why? Will not reason teach you sufficiently concerning God?

A. It will not.

Q. What? Is your understanding darkened by nature, and will not all the wisdom of the world lead you to the knowledge of God?

A. My understanding is darkened; and the world by wisdom knew not God. 1 Cor. i. 21.

C. True,

C. True, my dear children, and never could have known him, if it had not pleased God to reveal himself in his word. The works of God indeed bear a stamp upon them, that the hand which made them is divine, and in themselves are suited to prove the eternal power and godhead of their great Creator; but as the sun shines only to enlighten those who enjoy the faculty of vision, but conveys no gleam to the blind: so the works of creation and providence would still have left men without God in the world, if God had not revealed himself to us, and by traditionary notices, at first, and then by the Scriptures, preserved the knowledge of his being and perfections. Without this I greatly question whether fallen man, (notwithstanding the pride of philosophers) by any wisdom of his own, if left without tradition or the Scriptures, would know any more of God than the beasts which perish.

Q. How many Gods are there?

A. But one living and true God.

Q. How many persons are in the one godhead?

A. Three.

Q. The Unity in Trinity, and Trinity in Unity, is therefore to be worshipped?

A. So I believe.

Q. Do they who deny the three persons in the one godhead, know or worship the Scripture God?

A. They do not.

Q. Is

Q. Is the God, they worship who deny the Trinity, as much an idol of their imagination, as if they worshipped a stock or a stone?

A. Certainly. Eph. ii. 12.

C. True, my dear, for it matters not what kind of God men worship: if they know not the Scripture God, they are idolaters, nay, atheists, for to be without the true God, is, in fact, to have no God in the world.

Q. What names do these three persons in the godhead bear?

A. The names of Father, Son, and Holy Ghost.

Q. Are each of these by themselves to be worshipped as God and Lord?

A. They are.

Q. Are they in glory equal, and in majesty co-eternal?

A. So I believe.

Q. Then neither of them is before or after the other, neither greater nor less than the other.

A. This I steadfastly believe.

Q. Hath God a body, or parts of a body?

A. No.

Q. Is he a Spirit?

A. Yes.

Q. Is he possessed of infinite perfections?

A. He is.

Q. Is there none like unto God, or that can compare with him?

A. No,

A. No, in no wise.

Q. Is he *almighty* and able to do whatsoever pleaseth him?

A. Yes. Eccles. viii. 3.

Q. Is he every where present?

A. Yes, he filleth heaven and earth with his presence.

Q. Is he infinite in wisdom and knowledge?

A. He is.

Q. Do you think he knoweth the very secrets of your hearts?

A. I do. Psal. xliv. 21.

Q. Doth God know all that hath been, and all that shall be?

A. Yes. Known unto God from the beginning are all his works.

Q. Is he infinitely good and gracious?

A. Yes. His mercy is over all his works.

Q. Is he faithful and true to his promises?

A. Assuredly. None ever trusted him and were confounded.

Q. Is he infinitely just and righteous in all his works and ways?

A. He is.

Q. But when you have removed all possible imperfection from him, and ascribed to him all imaginable excellence, do you think you can attain unto the full and perfect knowledge of God, or is he above the thoughts of all created beings, incomprehensible? *A.* He

A. He is incomprehenſible. None can find out the Almighty to perfection.

Q. You ſay your knowledge of this bleſſed God is from the Scriptures, but can every perſon who reads the Scripture attain to this knowledge by the mere exerciſe of their natural reaſon?

A. No.

Q. Is there any ſupernatural aſſiſtance needful in order to underſtand the Scriptures?

A. There is. John vi. 45. Luke xxiv. 45.

Q. It is not by mere education or human teaching that you arrive at the knowledge of the true God, is it?

A. No. I muſt be taught of God.

Q. Cannot you underſtand the Scriptures without divine aſſiſtance?

A. Not to any ſaving purpoſe.

Q. Cannot a *natural* man with a good capacity, and human learning, underſtand the things which God's Spirit hath indited in his word?

A. No, in no wiſe. St. Paul ſaith, they appear fooliſhneſs to him, neither can he know them becauſe they are ſpiritually diſcerned.

Q. Muſt you look up therefore to be taught of God?

A. I muſt.

Q. And doth all the wiſdom which maketh wiſe to ſalvation, come from above, from the Father of lights?

A. It doth.

Q. May

Q. May a poor unlettered man, under divine teaching, know much more of the things of God, and the doctrines of truth, than the wisest unenlightened man, who leans only to his own understanding?

A. No doubt he may. Matt. xi. 25.

C. Well then, if this be the case, you see, poor, ignorant, and unlearned persons may know the true God, and the things that make for their everlasting peace, as well as the more polished part of mankind. Some of you perhaps may be neglected and not even taught to read your Bibles; but if you hear me or others who read and explain God's word unto you, and God gives you an understanding to receive the truth in the light and the love of it, manifesting himself to you as he doth not unto the world, you may be made a partaker of the faith of God's elect, and have a knowledge of Him, and his being, perfections, works and ways, which all the wisdom of a thousand Universities could never communicate to you. I speak not this to disparage seminaries of learning, or to encourage a careless neglect of so great an acquisition as knowledge. No. It is of all human things one of the most desirable, and a singular blessing to have enjoyed a good education. It was spoken to the honour of Moses that he was learned in all the wisdom of the Egyptians, but when this knowledge, as it often doth, puffs up the heart, and

men

men depend upon their own reason, and look for no higher teaching than men and books and study can communicate; then their wisdom becomes foolishness, their attainments are no better than splendid ignorance, and the meanest, most untutored Christian sees as much farther and deeper into the nature and perfections of the true God, and the things that make for his everlasting peace, as the light of the meridian sun discovers objects with a brightness surpassing that of the glimmering of the glow-worm.

VII.

C. We have been considering the first great object of faith, the triune God, he that cometh to God must believe that he is, according to his own revelation. You have told me, that in the unity of the godhead are three persons, Father, Son, and Holy Ghost. Which in order is first of these divine persons?

A. The Father.

Q. Is he God?

A. Yes. I believe the Father is God.

Q. What do you particularly believe concerning God the Father?

A. That he made me and all the world.

Q. Is not the world eternal?

A. No.

A. No.

Q. Had it a beginning?

A. Yes. In the beginning God created the heavens and the earth.

Q. What? Angels and men, and creatures of every kind?

A. Yes, all the host of them.

Q. So then from the highest archangel to the flie that is born and dies in a day, all are the work of God's hand?

A. They are.

Q. And is God the upholder and preserver of all?

A. Yes, in him they live and move, and have their being.

Q. Do all things depend upon his providence?

A. They do.

Q. Why do you give the title of Father to the first person of the sacred Trinity?

A. Chiefly because he is the Father of our Lord Jesus Christ.

Q. Do you not also regard God in the relation of a Father, *to you?*

A. Yes, he is my reconciled God and Father in Christ. Gal. iii. 26.

Q. Though God be the Creator of all, do some of his creatures stand in a nearer and more endeared relation to him than others?

A. They

A. They do.

Q. Hath he chosen them in Christ to be a kind of first fruits of his creatures?

A. He hath. Jam. i. 18.

Q. These therefore are called his elect, are they?

A. They are. Eph. i. 4, 5.

C. This first chapter of the Ephesians is well worthy of your serious perusal. I wish your parents, this evening, would read it over to you, for their own as well as your instruction and edification.

VIII.

C. We are considering the articles of our belief. The first of which is faith in God the Father Almighty, Maker of heaven and earth. In the divine essence he is the first divine person, and who is the second?

A. Jesus Christ his only Son our Lord.

Q. Is faith in Jesus Christ necessary to salvation?

A. Absolutely necessary. Acts xvi. 30, 31.

Q. Whosoever believeth not in him, must he, without doubt, perish everlastingly?

A. He must. John iii. 36.

Q. What is the meaning of the word Jesus?

A It

A. It signifies a Saviour. Matt. i. 21.

Q. Do you stand in need of a Saviour?

A. I do.

Q. Why? Are you a lost and helpless sinner?

A. Yes, wholly so. Rom. v. 6.

Q. Is Jesus come to seek and save that which is lost?

A. He is.

Q. You say you are a lost and helpless sinner, in need of a Saviour; do you think that for your sins you deserve to perish?

A. I do.

A. And can you make no compensation to God for them to obtain your pardon?

A. No, none at all. Psal. xlix. 7, 8.

Q. What? Are you by nature as weak as you are wicked?

A. I am wholly so. Rom. v. 6.

Q. Doth the guilt of sin condemn you—and the power of it enslave you?

A. It doth.

Q. And have you withal many spiritual enemies?

A. I have. The devil, the world, and my own wicked heart.

Q. Then you may well cry out with the apostle, Wretched man that I am, who shall deliver me? and here is the answer, I thank God, through

Jesus

Jesus Christ my Lord—Is it not a great mercy to have a Saviour to fly to in such a case?

A. Very great.

Q. And will not they be inexcusable who neglect so great a salvation?

A. No doubt they will be. Heb. ii. 3.

C. Take care then that it be not your own case, a Saviour is preached to you, able to the uttermost to rescue you from the curse and consequences of sin, from death and hell, and all your spiritual enemies. Believe in the Lord Jesus Christ, and you shall be saved. 'Tis faith in him alone can bring you victory over your fears and foes, and make you finally more than conquerors. I pray the Lord for you, that he may work it effectually in your hearts.

IX.

C. You have told me that you believe in Jesus the second person in the sacred Trinity, as your only, and all sufficient Saviour. We come now to consider the ground on which that faith is built: for it is not saying like the Roman governor, We have heard of *one Jesus*, that will do us any good, but being able to give a reason of the hope that is in us, and knowing that foundation to be everlastingly strong on which we build our confidence.

It is not babbling over the articles of our creed that makes us believers, but the understanding what we say, and having our hearts established in the truth as it is in Jesus, else our Christianity is but an empty name, and our profession of faith, but as sounding brass and tinkling cymbal.

Q. Do you believe in Jesus then as *the Christ?*

A. I do.

Q. What is the meaning of the word Jesus?

A. It signifies anointed.

C. Messiah, Christ, Anointed, are all words of the same meaning, only in different languages. Jesus is the true Messiah, anointed of God, and thereby both appointed by the divine will, and qualified by the divine Spirit, for the execution of the work of our salvation. Can you tell me who were by God's command under the Old Testament appointed to be anointed for their offices?

A. Prophets, priests, and kings.

Q. You are right, and they were herein the types and figures of him who united all these offices in his own person, and is therefore by way of eminence stiled, *The Christ.*

Q. Is Christ your *Prophet?*

A. He is. Deut. xviii. 15.

Q. Was it the prophet's office to teach the mind and will of God to the people?

A. It was.

Q. Do

Q. Do you want a divine prophet and teacher?
A. I do.
Q. Is there great blindness and spiritual ignorance in your natural understanding?
A. There is.   Eph. iv. 18.
Q. And can no teaching but that of Jesus Christ effectually remove it?
A. No other can be effectual.   1 Cor. i. 21.
Q. Would you never know or feel the true state of guilt and misery in which you are born and live by nature, if Jesus did not teach you?
A. I should not.   2 Cor. iv. 6.   John xvi. 8.
Q. But do not people readily confess they are sinners?
A. They do.
Q. But is there not a great difference between mens general confessions of sin, and a real feeling conviction of it on the conscience?
A. Great difference indeed.
Q. Must the Spirit of Jesus give you a divine conviction of sin, before you can confess it to any saving purpose?
A. He must, or my confessions will be otherwise mere words.
Q. Can you savingly know any of the truths of God without this anointed Prophet's help?
A. No, he must lead me into *all* truth.

C. I

C. I pray God for you, my dear children, that he may, and that you may know him to be your prophet by blessed heart-felt experience.

Q. What is the second office which Christ the anointed bears?

A. That of Priest.

Q. Was it the office of the priest under the law to offer up sacrifices for the peoples sins?

A. It was. Heb. viii. 3.

Q. And did he pray for them, that God would accept the blood of atonement of the beast which was slain, and pardon, bless, and save them?

A. He did.

Q. Do you think that in this the priest was a type and figure of Christ?

A. He was. Heb. ix. 9.

Q. Hath Jesus Christ offered up to God the Father any sacrifice for sin?

A. Yes, himself. Heb. vii. 27.

Q. And doth he ever live to pray and make intercession for us?

A. He doth. Heb. vii. 25.

Q. Do we want such an High-Priest?

A. Oh yes, exceedingly.

Q. What would become of us if he had not offered up himself for us?

A. We must have perished. John xi. 50.

Q. And

Q. And could we ever now approach God with acceptance, if we had not Jesus as our advocate with the Father?

A. We could not. John xiv. 6.

Q. So then all our hopes of pardon for our sins, and every answer to our prayers, depend entirely upon the sacrifice and intercession of our High-Priest, Christ Jesus.

A. They do.

Q. What is the third office to which Jesus is anointed?

A. To be *the King* of his people.

Q. Is it the office of a king to defend his subjects from their enemies?

A. It is.

Q. Do you think that Jesus your anointed King is able and willing to put all your spiritual enemies under your feet?

A. I do. Luke i. 71.

Q. Are you bound to pray to him, and depend upon him for this purpose?

A. No doubt I am. Psal. xxii. 5.

Q. And is this the true exercise of faith in him as your Saviour Christ?

A. It is.

Q. Is it the office of a king to confer favours and honours on his subjects?

A. Yes.

Q. Hath the Lord Jesus any favours and honours to confer?

A. He hath, the greatest imaginable.

Q. Doth he give grace and glory?

A. He doth.

Q. And shall his people live and reign as kings and priests with him in heaven?

A. So hath he promised. Rev. i. 6.

Q. You say Christ is thus anointed to be the Prophet, Priest, and King of his people, when did God thus solemnly consecrate and set him apart for these offices?

A. At his baptism.

Q. Did God give any visible and miraculous sign of his consecration?

A. Yes. The Spirit of God as a dove descended from heaven upon him.

Q. And did God the Father audibly proclaim him to the world?

A. Yes. There came a voice from heaven, saying, This is my beloved Son in whom I am well pleased.

Q. Did Jesus as the anointed, receive any qualification for the discharge of the great offices, to which God the Father thus gloriously appointed him?

A. Yes, the Father gave not the Spirit by measure unto him.

Q. Do

Q. Do you believe he received from the Father in his human nature all fulness of grace, wisdom, and power, to enable him to finish the work which he had given him to do?

A. I do.

C. I hope you do, and that every day, through an increasing acquaintance with the Scriptures, you will be going on to the full assurance of hope unto the end. It is a great thing to believe. God alone can bestow this heavenly gift on the heart. I can instruct you, and you may hear me, and understand the import of the words, but it is God must give you to believe. Confession with the lip and tongue that Jesus is the Christ, is easily made, but experimentally to know him to be such, is a divine work in the heart; we may speak and hear of him as a Prophet, Priest, and King; but it is of the unsearchable riches of his grace, if you and I are by him as our Prophet, brought out of nature's darkness into God's marvellous light, if we are enabled to take him as our Priest, flying to his blood and righteousness, and intercession for peace and acceptance with God under all our guilt, corruption, and backslidings, and to commit our souls to him as our King, to be protected, comforted, saved from all our fears and foes. Therefore, least we should take up with forms of words or vain profession, instead of experimental knowledge, doth

St. John so awfully warn us, that no man can say that Jesus is the Christ, but by the Holy Ghost.

X.

Q. Whose Son is Jesus Christ?

A. The Son of God. Matt. xvi. 16.

Q. Are there not other sons of God besides? are not angels and men called so in Scripture?

A. They are.

Q. Is Christ the Son of God in a peculiar sense to which no creature can pretend?

A. He is. Matt. xi. 27.

Q. Is he therefore distinguished as God's *only* Son?

A. Yes, he is the only begotten of the Father.

Q. Are the Father and Son one in the glory of the undivided Godhead?

A. They are. John x. 30.

C. This mysterious union is far above our comprehension, and our finite knowledge cannot declare his generation. One thing only we are assured of in Scripture, that He is very God of very God, the same with the Father in nature, substance, and glory. That he was in the beginning with God, and was God; that he is the true God; is in the form of God; equal with God; and distinguished by the same names, titles, and attributes as the Father; known by the same works of creation and providence, and claiming the same worship and honour from angels in heaven, and men upon earth. So that either Jesus Christ, is, as the only Son of the Father, God over all, blessed for ever, or the Scriptures deceive us, for either they reveal to us no God at all, or Jesus Christ is that God.

Q. Do you think it of the highest importance to be grounded in the faith of this truth?

A. I do.

C. No doubt it is most important to believe this; for on the glory of the Godhead of the Son depends all the sufficiency of his undertaking. Less than God manifest in the flesh, he had been unable to make an end of sin, to finish transgression, and bring in everlasting righteousness. To accomplish these great ends it became necessary, that he by *the eternal Spirit* should in our stead offer himself without spot unto God. And *as God* he purchased the church with his own blood. All guilty fears and doubts vanish, and solid confidence, hope and peace, spring up in the conscience, when knowing in whom we have believed, our souls repose on the incarnate Jehovah.

Q. Is the name Jehovah peculiar to the most high God?

A. It is.

Q. Is this name ever given to Jesus Christ?

A. Yes.

A. Yes. Exod. xix. 3. to the 17th verse, compared with Acts vii. 38.—And again, Isa. vi. 1. to the 5th verse, compared with John xii. 41.

C. Your proofs are pertinent and strong. And what is very remarkable, these two passages, where the Jehovah of the Old Testament is expresly said to be Jesus Christ in the New, contain two of the most glorious manifestations, which God ever made of himself under that dispensation. The one on Mount Sinai, when the law was given, the other to Isaiah, who may very well be stiled the prince of the prophets.

Q. Is Christ stiled God in Scripture?

A. He is. John i. 1. 1 John v. 20. John xx. 28. Rom. ix. 5.

Q. Is he called Lord also?

A. He is. John xxviii. 28.

Q. Are the *attributes* of deity ascribed to him, as almighty[a], eternal[b], self-existent[c], omniscient[d], omnipresent[e]?

A. They are.

Q. Are the peculiar works of God, those of creation and providence, attributed to him?

A. They are. Col. i. 16, 17. John i. 3. Heb. i. 3.

---

[a] Rev. i. 8.　　[b] Psal. xc. 2.　　[c] John viii. 5.
[d] Acts i. 24.　　[e] Matt. xviii. 20.

Q. Doth

Q. Doth he claim the prerogative of forgiving sins, and anfwering the prayers of his people, and giving life eternal?

A. He doth. Matt. ix. 2—6. Mark. xi. 7. Matt. xxi. 22. John v. 21. John v. 19.

Q. Doth he claim and receive equal honours and worfhip with the Father?

A. He does. Phil. xi. 6. John x. 30. xiv. 9, 10. v. 23. Heb. i. 6.

Q. And is this worfhip and honour paid him by angels and men?

A. It is. Ifa. vi. 1—5. Rev. iv. 8. vi. 10. Acts vii. 59.

Q. Doth all this, collectively taken, prove Jefus Chrift to be very God?

A. Without all doubt it doth.

Q. Would it be the higheft blafphemy to afcribe to him thefe divine honours and pay him this worfhip if he were not very God?

A. It would be fo.

Q. If he be thus infinitely glorious in his nature, you ought to place the firmeft confidence in his work as your Saviour, ought you not?

A. I fhould do fo.

C. I pray God that you may, and be enabled with comfort to commit your poor and finful foul to the pardoning love and gracious care of your Saviour

Saviour and your God. Then through the mercy of the moſt Higheſt you ſhall not miſcarry.

XI.

C. You profeſs to believe in Jeſus Chriſt the only Son of God, as one in nature, and of one ſubſtance with the Father, what relation doth he particularly bear towards you, and what eſpecial intereſt have you in him?

A. He is *our Lord*.

Q. Is he conſtituted and appointed Lord of all things?

A. He is. Heb. i. 2.

Q. Doth he, as Mediator, enjoy this particular power and authority, for the good of his church and people?

A. He doth.

Q. Is all created nature put under his feet?

A. It is. He doth whatſoever pleaſeth him in the hoſts of heaven, and among the inhabitants of the earth.

Q. All muſt bow before him therefore, whether they will or no; but have ſome a nearer relation to him than others?

A. Yes, his redeemed people.

Q. Are they peculiarly his care?

A. They are. Mal. iii. 17.

Q. Is

Q. Is he their guardian and protector?

A. He is. Isa. xxvii. 3.

Q. Is he the Lord our righteousness?

A. So he is called. Jer. xxiii. 6.

Q. Must we be found in his divine righteousness, if we would stand complete before the throne of God?

A. We must, and in this righteousness only. Phil. iii. 9.

Q. If he is our Lord, ought we not to trust him as near to help in every time of need?

A. Certainly. Psal. cxlv. 18.

Q. And hath he not a right to our first affections, and chearful service?

A. Assuredly he hath. Psal. xxxi. 23.

Q. But do not many say, Lord, Lord, who very much neglect the commands of Jesus Christ?

A. They too often do.

Q. Then it is not every one that saith, Lord, Lord, who enters into the kingdom of heaven?

A. No. Matt. vii. 21.

Q. What will be the end of those who confess him in words, and deny him by wicked works?

A. They must without all doubt perish everlastingly. Matt. vii. 23.

Q. Ought you not therefore betimes to think about loving, serving, and pleasing Jesus Christ our Lord?

A. I

A. I ought to do so.

C. My dear children, I hope through the grace of God you will do so: and not merely learn by rote the words of your creed, but feel and evidence the influence of divine faith upon your hearts by your works; yielding up body, soul and spirit, to the service of your liege Lord and gracious master Jesus Christ.

XII.

C. We have been considering the Godhead and glory of our Redeemer and Saviour Jesus Christ, whom truly to know is everlasting life. We come now to the consideration of his human nature, in which united to the divine he fulfilled the great work of the sinner's salvation, and as God and man in one Christ now lives and reigns for ever and ever, to the comfort of his chosen, and to the confusion of his enemies. It was needful in making peace between an offended holy God, and the sinful sons of men, that the person who undertook to be the repairer of the breach should partake of both natures, and be a proper daysman, as Job calls him, to lay his hand upon us both. In our nature, as a surety to satisfy the righteous demands of God's justice and holy law, and as God-man, to give to his sacrifice and obedience, when he became incarnate

nate for us men, and for our salvation, that transcendent excellence, completeness, and all-sufficiency, that the Father, well-pleased for his righteousness sake, and glorified in the highest by the work of our great surety, might, consistent with his own perfections justify, sanctify, and glorify, through the riches of his grace, those who in themselves were ill-deserving, yea hell-deserving, helpless, and desperate. Proceed we therefore to the incarnation, sufferings, death, resurrection, and mediatorial glory of our God and Saviour Jesus Christ.

Q. Was God's only Son, our Lord, incarnate and made flesh?

A. He was. John i. 14.

Q. Had he a human body and reasonable soul, just as the other children of men?

A. He had, being in all things made like unto his brethren. Heb. ii. 14.

Q. One thing only excepted. All the sons and daughters of Adam are conceived in sin and born in wickedness, but was the Son of God?

A. No, in him was no sin.

Q. By what means was this ordered, that he should take our nature without the sin which had corrupted it throughout?

A. He was conceived of the Holy Ghost, and born of the Virgin Mary.

Q. Was

Q. Was it necessary that he who in our nature was to make atonement for others, should himself be without sin?

A. It was. 1 John iii. 5. Heb. vii. 26.

Q. Had sin been found in him, he would not have been a Lamb without spot or blemish, to take away the sin of the world. Was it also necessary that the human nature of Christ should be thus holy, harmless, undefiled, and separate from sinners, in order to be taken into personal union with the uncreated *WORD*?

A. It was.

Q. Do you believe that by the miraculous and inconceivable agency of the Holy Ghost, a body was prepared from the Virgin Mary, of spotless purity, and inseparably united with the person of the Son of God?

A. That is my faith. Luke i. 35.

Q. Was the Virgin Mary a Jewess?

A. Yes.

Q. And were not herself, and husband Joseph, both of the royal house and lineage of David?

A. They were. Luke ii. 4.

Q. Had God promised to David, that of the fruit of his loins, the Messiah should spring?

A. He had. Acts ii. 30.

Q. Did not Joseph and Mary go up to Bethlehem, David's city, to be taxed?

A. They

A. They did.

Q. That was a proof, therefore, they were his descendants; and was Christ born at Bethlehem?

A. He was.

Q. Had it been foretold that so it should be?

A. It had. Micah v. 2.

Q. In what sort of place was Christ brought forth?

A. In a stable: because there was no room for them at the inn.

Q. Was not this a vast instance of humility, that the Son of God should stoop so low as to take our nature, and with such abasing circumstances?

A. It was.

Q. Ought we not to follow the example of his great humility?

A. We ought assuredly to do so.

Q. Does not this condemn all who murmur and repine at their poverty and low estate?

A. It doth.

C. Well, take notice of the child Jesus, my dear children, and learn to be pleased with your station. The meanest of you hath a better house to cover you then he was born in. His cradle was a manger; his father a poor carpenter; and when he grew up, he had not where to lay his head. Oh how should the view of the humiliation of Jesus reconcile us to every condition, sweeten our lot wherever God hath

hath caft it, and teach us, in whatever ftate we are, therewith to be content.

XIII.

C. We have been confidering the incarnation of the Son of God, that amazing work, which angels with aftonifhment, defire to look into, admiring and adoring the condefcenfion of our Immanuel. He bowed the heavens and came down, and took upon him the nature of man, and being found in fafhion as a man, he humbled himfelf. Oh the depths of his love! He humbled himfelf to death, even the death of the crofs. He became man for our falvation, he took our nature that he might bear our iniquities, and in the place of finners fuffer, what we had deferved: making atonement by his blood; fatisfying the juftice of a holy God; and purchafing by his obedience unto death, even the death of the crofs, that life and glory, which we by fin had forfeited, and through our defperate corruption were for ever unable to regain. Tell me therefore,

Q. Do you believe that Jefus Chrift fuffered?
A. I do.
Q. Under whom?
A. Pontius Pilate.

Q. Was

Q. Was he at that time the Roman governour of Judea?

A. He was.

Q. What kind of suffering did Christ undergo?

A. He was crucified.

Q. Was he nailed to the cross as the vilest of malefactors?

A. Yes.

Q. Was crucifixion a most shameful—painful—and accursed death?

A. It was.

Q. Had we deserved to suffer for our sins eternal shame, and torment, and the curse of God?

A. We had, most justly.

Q. Did Jesus Christ in his own person undertake to bear this dreadful burthen for us?

A. He did. Isa. liii. 5.

Q. And did God the Father lay upon him the iniquity of us all?

A. Yes, of us all. Isa. liii. 6.

Q. Did he die the just for the unjust?

A. He did. 1 Pet. iii. 18.

Q. Are all the sins of the redeemed paid for in the precious drops of Jesus' blood?

A. They are. 1 Pet. i. 18, 19.

Q. If the Lord then took him as our surety, and accepted his offering as our ransom, is it righteous and just in God the Father to forgive us our sins?

A. It

A. It is. 1 John i. 9.

Q. Is he bound by his own justice to pardon the believer in Jesus?

A. He is. He hath accepted the surety for the sinner.

Q. Could nothing short of this price ransom us from our iniquities?

A. Nothing. Acts iv. 12.

Q. The cross of Christ in this view shews us in the strongest light the dreadful nature of sin, doth it not?

A. It doth.

Q. Did Christ die upon the cross?

A. Yes.

Q. Was it necessary that he should die?

A. It was. Heb. ii. 14.

Q. Was death the wages of sin?

A. It was.

Q. And did Christ by the grace of God taste of death for every one of his redeemed?

A. He did.

Q. What is the sting of death?

A. Sin.

Q. Hath Christ taken away that sting?

A. He hath. 1 Cor. 15. 57.

Q. Ought a believer in Jesus now to be afraid of death?

A. No. In no wise. Rom. viii. 37.

Q. Who

Q. Who hath the power of death?

A. The devil.

Q. Hath Christ destroyed the devil's power, by dying for us?

A. He hath. Heb. ii. 14.

Q. Is the serpent's head broken by the bruised heel of Jesus?

A. It is. Gen. iii. 15.

Q. Is it not a great comfort to be able to triumph over sin, satan, death, and hell?

A. The greatest in the world.

Q. And what is it, that gives us this victory?

A. Our faith.

Q. But have all men faith?

A. No. 2 Thess. iii. 2.

Q. Do not many who call themselves believers, deceive themselves?

A. Yes, greatly. Rev. iii. 9.

Q. Do they not live under the guilt and power of sin, and the fear of death?

A. They do.

Q. Hath Christ for them died in vain?

A. He hath.

C. Remember this, my dear children, it is not every one who talks of a crucified Jesus that really believes on him. They who know nothing of the evil of sin, for which he died,—they who live contentedly under the power of sin—they who never

felt

felt their hearts pierced with a sense of the Redeemer's sufferings—they who have not yet learned to loath themselves and sin—never truly knew or believed in a dying Redeemer! May a sense of his amazing grace affect your consciences! May you be enabled to look on him whom they have pierced and mourn! May you find the efficacy of his cross in your hearts! May you be enabled to glory in it daily! Triumphing over guilt — treading down satan as a vanquished foe—defying death and its sting—and looking forward with joyful hope, in the confidence, that to live is Christ, and to die is gain.

XIV.

C. The humiliations of the Son of God have been the subject of our last lecture: and such humiliations as every time we reflect upon them, should fill our inmost souls with deepest abasement, and warmest gratitude towards him. By his sufferings we are eased; by his stripes we are healed; by his death we have life. But for him our state had been as fearful and desperate as that of devils: By him we have now secured to us bliss and blessedness equal, perhaps superior, to that of angels. Though we must follow our master through the grave, the gate of death, he hath trod the path, the

the marks of his footsteps are seen there, and he saith to us, as to the patriarch going down into Egypt, fear not to go down; I will go down with thee, and I will surely bring thee up again. This will make the consideration of the next article of the creed comfortable to us.

Q. Was the body of Jesus buried when it was taken from the cross?

A. Yes.

Q. Was it laid in a tomb hewn out of a rock, where nobody had been ever laid?

A. It was. Luke xxiii. 53.

Q. What became of the human soul of Jesus?

A. It went to Paradise. Luke xxiii. 43.

Q. Is this what you mean by descending into hell, or hades?

A. Yes.

Q. You do not suppose that the soul of Jesus actually entered into the place and state of the damned?

A. No.

Q. Had he finished the work of suffering on the cross?

A. He had. John xix. 30.

Q. You believe, therefore, that in death the body and soul of Jesus underwent the same change as do all his people?

A. I do.

Q. Must

Q. Muſt your body and ſoul be ſhortly ſeparated by death?

A. They muſt.

Q. Muſt the grave be the place of your abode?

A. Yes, aſſuredly.

Q. Is it not natural for us to dread this ſeparation of body and ſoul?

A. Very natural.

Q. Don't you ſhudder when you look into a grave and ſee the duſt and rotten bones, like to which you muſt ſhortly be?

A. Yes.

Q. Will it not be very deſireable to know how to overcome theſe fears?

A. Very deſireable.

C. Well then, look to the livid corpſe of Jeſus, laid in the cold tomb; this will perfume that pit of putrefaction, and open in the grave a door of hope. The bed of clay, is now become a bed of roſes, and like the ſweet ſleep of a labouring man. Death will be to a believer in Jeſus, a gentle ſhort repoſe, from whence in the reſurrection day he will riſe refreſhed, and blooming in all the vigour of immortal health and beauty.

XV.

The Scriptures which spake of the sufferings of Jesus, we have seen fulfilled in his crucifixion, death and burial. We proceed now to the glory which they had foretold, should shortly follow; it being determined and engaged for in the everlasting covenant, that God the Father would not leave his soul in hell, nor suffer his Holy One to see corruption; the path of life was to be shewn him through the grave, and Jesus, the conquering Jesus was appointed to lead his captivity captive. When he entered, the territories of death, as his people's representative, it was not to lie down among the slain, but to vanquish for them, and binding this king of terrors as a captive foe, to rise the conqueror of death and hell, and openly proclaim his victory, to the exaltation of his own honour, and for their eternal comfort and triumph.

Q. How long lay the body of Jesus in the grave?

A. Part of three days. Friday evening, all Saturday, and till Sunday morning.

Q. Did he rise the third day according to the Scriptures?

A. He did.

Q. Have we the strongest evidence imaginable of this truth, that Jesus rose again?

A. We

A. We have.

Q. And was it needful we should?

A. Yes.

Q. Did much depend upon it?

A. Yes. Our whole salvation.

Q. Is this the hinge upon which the great proof turns, that Jesus Christ is our Saviour?

A. It is.

Q. If Christ be not risen from the dead, is our preaching vain, and faith vain, are we yet in our sins?

A. We are. 1 Cor. xv. 17.

Q. Did Christ go into the grave as a public person, as the representative and surety for his people?

A. He did.

Q. If he had not risen, could we hope that our ransom was paid, and his suffering accepted?

A. We could not.

Q. But is the matter now certain, that God for his sake justifies the ungodly?

A. Yes. He was delivered for our offences, and raised again for our justification.

Q. Can nothing now condemn those for whom Christ died?

A. Nothing. They are justified from all things, and shall never enter into condemnation, but are passed from death unto life.

Q. If

Q. If it was so important to us that Jesus should rise again, ought we not to be well acquainted with the proofs of his resurrection?

A. Surely, we ought.

Q. Is our faith built upon this evidence?

A. It is.

Q. Ought every one who calls himself a believer, to be able to give a reason of the hope that is in him?

A. Certainly he ought.

C. Acquaint yourselves therefore with the Scriptures, that you may not merely repeat your creed, but feel the conviction which arises from the fullest evidence of the truth.

Q. Was every possible precaution taken by the murderers of Jesus, to prove him an impostor?

A. Yes.

Q. Did they not make the sepulchre as sure as they could, placing a guard of soldiers at the entrance, rolling a great stone to the door, and setting the public seal upon it?

A. They did.

C. They were in hopes on the third day to take the body out of the grave, and shewing it to the people, to prove Jesus a deceiver; because he rested the proof of his mission and doctrine upon his resurrection; for he had said to them, when they demanded evidence of his being sent from God as the true Messiah, Destroy this temple, pointing to his body, and in three days I will raise it up again.

Q. What was become of Christ's disciples when he was seized and executed?

A. They all forsook him and fled.

Q. Was there any danger of their attempting to rescue the body?

A. None in the world.

Q. Could they have reaped any advantage from the attempt if they had succeeded.

A. No. In no wise.

Q. Then they had no interest to propagate a delusion?

A. No. If they had not the fullest conviction of the fact themselves, they must have been of all men most miserable to have asserted it.

Q. Did the precautions that had been taken serve the stronger to prove the fact of the resurrection?

A. Yes, in the strongest manner.

Q. Who were the first witnesses of the resurrection?

A. The soldiers who guarded the body.

Q. Can you tell me any of the circumstances?

A. Yes. There was a great earthquake. An angel of the Lord descended from heaven in glory, and rolled the stone from the grave,—and the keepers were so terrified and affrighted, that they
deserted

deserted their post, and ran into the city and told what they had seen.

Q. Were not the high priests and pharisees very desirous to smother their report?

A. They were.

Q. Did they give them a large sum of money, and a promise to screen them from the governour's anger for deserting their post, if they would tell a lie?

A. They did.

Q. And what was the lie they put in the soldiers mouth?

A. That Jesus's disciples came by night, whilst they slept, and stole him away.

C. How improbable a story, how impracticable an attempt! Would a whole band of soldiers be asleep at once: asleep when such a charge was committed to them—asleep, when if found sleeping they knew they would be put to death by their military laws!—If one or another slumber'd, would many, would the whole band, all fall asleep—all at the same time? And were the disciples men so daring as to attempt a rescue in the face of danger so imminent! Those cowards who, when their master was alive forsook him and fled—even the most zealous and courageous of them all, Peter, so frighted when only questioned by a servant maid, that he denied him, yea, cursed and swore he never

E   knew

knew him: would these at the hazard of their lives, nay, almost with a certainty of death before them, dare to approach the sepulchre? Could they hope to find a whole band of soldiers so negligent as to be all asleep? Could they dare even if that was the case, to pass through the midst of them, break open the sepulchre, roll back a vast stone that required so great strength to remove, fetch out the dead body, and carry it off, and make no noise, not awake one of this numerous guard?—How credulous must they be who could entertain such a suggestion?—Infidels always are constrained to believe more than even God's word requires of his people, though they dare so often ridicule the followers of Jesus as credulous. But what interest had the disciples to do this? Could they gain their ends, and have the resurrection credited, were they likely to receive benefit by the delusion? Just the very contrary; shame, contempt, poverty, disgrace, hatred, sufferings of every kind, yea, the most tormenting deaths were to be the certain rsuit of their testimony? Could ever man in his senses take such a step. Would multitudes thus expose themselves without the fullest conviction of the truth which they asserted, and the importance of it to their own eternal happiness, and that of mankind?—So far we hear the first evidence.

Q. Who

Q. Who are next evidences of the resurrection of Jesus?

A. His disciples.

Q. Did they see him after he rose?

A. Yes, many times.

Q. How long?

A. During forty days.

Q. Were they numerous or few?

A. A great many.

Q. How many at one time saw him?

A. Above five hundred.

Q. Did they converse, and eat and drink with him?

A. They did.

Q. Might they not be mistaken in the person?

A. No. Certainly not.

Q. Did the strangeness of the thing, and the weight of the consequences flowing from it, make them require the strongest proof of Jesus, that it was he himself?

A. It did.

Q. Did Jesus graciously satisfy their doubts, silence their unbelief, and give them full conviction that he was the very person after his resurrection, whom they had seen suffer on the cross?

A. He did.

Q. By what means?

A. He

A. He conversed, eat and drank with them during forty days, and to remove all possibility of doubt, he shewed them his hands where the nails had fastened him to the cross, and his side where the soldiers spear had entered into his heart, and bid them feel the marks, and be convinced that it was no phantom but real flesh and bones, even he himself their former and well known master.

Q. Were they all convinced of the truth?

A. They were.

Q. Did they give the strongest evidence that they were so by sealing it with their blood?

A. They did.

Q. Then we have the fullest evidence that they could not be imposed upon themselves, and have given us the strongest proof that man can give, that they meant not to impose upon others?

A. We have, to the utmost.

Q. Did the angels from heaven bear testimony to this fact?

A. They did. Luke xxiv. 6.

Q. Did God also himself set his seal to this truth?

A. Yes.

Q. How.

A. By the signs and miracles which the first preachers of the gospel were enabled to work in

proof·

proof of the truth which they advanced. Mark xvi. 20.

Q. Have we ourselves any present proof of the fact in our own experience?

A. We have.

Q. Was the gift of the Holy Ghost on the day of pentecost, and are all the gifts and graces of the Spirit now bestowed on the redeemed, evident proofs that Jesus is alive for evermore?

A. They are. Acts ii. 33.

Q. Then our faith doth not rest merely on outward evidence however strong or forcible, every true believer hath the witness in himself, hath he not?

A. He hath. 1 John v. 10.

C. Mind this, my dear children. Men may learn to talk of the resurrection of Jesus, and learned men may support it by these arguments which I have advanced, and many others; but if we are only taught of men, and rest upon human reasonings merely, our faith standing only on the wisdom of men and not on the power of God, will not endure the test in the day of trial. We must have the internal evidence of the resurrection of Jesus in our hearts, as quickened by his Spirit from the death of sin unto the life of righteousness, and then we shall be able with divine evidence to say, I know in whom I have believed. This is that faith of God's operation that is peculiar to the redeemed and inseparable from salvation. I pray God that you may be possessed of this unspeakable gift, and whilst you are enabled to give a pertinent answer to him that asketh you a reason of the hope that is in you, that you may enjoy a still fuller evidence in your own conscience, than the strongest arguments, and most conclusive reasoning can convey to others, even the answer of a good conscience towards God, through the resurrection of Jesus from death, having inward experience of the fact from this blessed effect produced by his Spirit in your hearts.

XVI.

Q. How long did our Lord Jesus continue upon earth after his resurrection?

A. Forty days.

Q. What became of him afterwards?

A. He ascended into heaven.

Q. Who saw him ascend?

A. His disciples.

Q. How did he ascend?

A. His body went up, till a cloud received him out of their sight.

Q. Did Christ go up into heaven as the head and representative of his chosen people?

A. He

A. He did. Heb. vi. 20.

Q. Then it was needful *for us* that he should go thither?

A. So he assures us. John xvi. 7.

Q. Hath he by entering into heaven for us, opened the kingdom of heaven to all believers?

A. He hath.

Q. Were we by sin excluded from God's presence?

A. We were. Heb. i. 13.

Q. But have we now access to the holiest of all through the blood of Jesus?

A. We have. Heb. x. 19.

Q. Has he promised to go before to prepare a place for us?

A. He hath promised so to do. John xiv. 2.

Q. And will he fulfil it?

A. I trust he will.

Q. Then you expect to be with him where he is, to behold his glory?

A. I do.

Q. But will not all your manifold iniquities prevent you?

A. No. There is no condemnation to them that are in Christ Jesus. They cannot perish for whom he died, and rose again. Rom. viii. 1.

Q. Did Christ promise to send to his disciples a comforter after he was gone?

A. He

A. He did.   John xvi. 7.

Q. Who is that comforter?

A. The Holy Ghost.

Q. And did Christ send him?

A. Yes.   At the day of pentecost.

Q. Besides the miraculous gifts of the Spirit which he then gave unto men, doth he continue to minister to all his people the same Spirit for their comfort, light, and sanctification?

A. He doth.   Matt. xxviii. 20. Rom. viii. 9.

Q. Are you to expect the same Spirit to be sent into your hearts, as was given to the primitive Christians?

A. Assuredly.   1 Cor. xii. 13.

Q. Is his influence as necessary for every good work now, as it was to inable the apostles to work miracles then?

A. It is.   John xv. 5.

Q. Has Christ taken possession on your behalf of the heavenly inheritance?

A. He hath.   Eph. ii. 6.

Q. Then all your title to glory depends on his finished work?

A. Entirely.   Phil. iii. 9. Col. ii. 10.

Q. Do you expect to be with Christ on account of your own goodness, or merely through the riches of his grace?

A. By grace; only by grace I am saved.

Q. Is

Q. Is Chriſt gone up as a conqueror?

A. Yes. He hath led my captivity captive.

Q. Then all your foes are really vanquiſhed?

A. They are.

Q. Can any of them now pluck you out of the all-conquering Jeſus' hand?

A. No. None. John x. 28.

Q. Then your redemption in him is now compleat and everlaſting?

A. It is. Heb. ix. 12.

Q. If this be true, ought you not in affection to be following Chriſt into the heavens?

A. Yes. I am bound to do ſo.

Q. Should your heart be now with him?

A. Certainly. Col. iii. 1, 2.

Q. Ought you confidently to truſt upon him as your captain, leading you aſſuredly to conqueſt and a crown?

A. I ought to do ſo.

Q. Is this the honour he expects from his people, that they ſhould thus truſt and not be afraid?

A. It is.

Q. Is it your duty and privilege to draw near to Jeſus in the heavens, to receive out of his fulneſs the gifts which he now hath to beſtow?

A. It is my bounden duty, and higheſt privilege.

E 5 *Q.* And

Q. And will he assuredly give his Holy Spirit to them that ask him?

A. Yes, as surely as he is in heaven.

C. Well, my dear children, see that you correspond in practice with these your professions. It is not confessing Christ in word and tongue, but in deed and in truth, which can prove us real believers of his ascension into heaven. Many pretend to say they believe him to be there, whose affections are set upon things on earth, not in heaven: many say he hath led captivity captive, who continue serving divers lusts and pleasures: many talk of the gifts of his Spirit, whose hearts remain totally unrenewed, and whose spirit is earthly, sensual, devilish. These give the lie in works to the professions they make, and shew that they have as yet no visible part in the kingdom of God and of Christ. But I hope better things of you, that you will early remember your blessed Master, and, as one of our own gracious collects has taught us, be without ceasing found at his footstool in prayer for his Spirit to raise your affections to high and heavenly things, and in heart and mind thither ascend, where Jesus Christ is gone before.

XVII.

We have seen the mighty Jesus ascending to the glorious abode, from whence in love to us men,

and

and for our salvation, he had come down. May we ever in heart follow him thither, till the blessed season arrives when he shall take us to his kingdom, to live and reign with him for ever. He is himself set down on his throne, and has engaged to bring us to sit down with him in glory everlasting.

Q. Where is Jesus Christ at present?

A. He sitteth at the right hand of God the Father Almighty.

Q. Is he as man, the mediator, exalted of his Father to this state of transcendant dignity?

A. He is. Because he humbled himself to death, even the death of the cross, therefore God hath highly exalted him, and given him a name above every name.

Q. In his divine nature he could not be exalted, being in himself God over all, blessed for ever, you mean he is exalted in his office-character as mediator?

A. I do so.

C. When he is said to be in one place at the right hand of God, we mean not that his Godhead can be circumscribed. He filleth heaven and earth with his presence. But as mediator he is now at the right hand of God, put in full possession of all the spiritual blessings in heavenly things for his people's use, and from thence he dispenses sovereignly to them according to their wants, and the good pleasure of his will. Tell me then particularly, who

furnishes

furnishes his ministers and people with gifts and graces for all the work and service, to which he calls them?

A. Jesus at the right hand of God.

Q. Is he also there appearing in the presence of God for us as an advocate, if any man sin?

A. He is. 1 John ii. 1.

Q. And is it in virtue of his pleading for us that we find favour with God?

A. Entirely so. Rom. viii. 33, 34.

Q. Doth he there pray for his people?

A. Yes, he ever liveth to make intercession for us.

Q. Are we not also bound to pray for ourselves?

A. Undoubtedly. He hath injoined us so to do.

Q. But would our prayers have any effect, or enter into heaven if he did not present them before the throne?

A. No. The prayers of God's saints ascend up before God, out of the great angel's hands, with his incense. Rev. viii. 3.

Q. Then we can only receive an answer of peace, when we pray in faith, looking unto Jesus?

A. Without this, all our prayers would be wholly ineffectual. John xiv. 6.

Q. Are we now sure of being heard when we pray?

A. Yes.

A. Yes. Whatsoever we ask in Christ's name, believing, we shall receive.

Q. Is not this the strongest encouragement, to be much and often in this blessed work?

A. It is. Christ's people should always pray and not faint.

Q. Is Christ at the right hand of God also Lord of all?

A. He is. He hath now taken the kingdom for his own, and all power is given to him in heaven and on earth.

Q. Must all his enemies lick the dust?

A. They must.

Q. Then satan, sin, death, and hell, can do nothing against Jesus on the throne?

A. No. They are vanquished foes.

Q. Doth Christ always make his people to triumph?

A. It is their privilege to do so. 2 Cor. ii. 14.

Q. Hath he power to forgive sins?

A. He hath. Matt. ix. 6.

Q. Then we may trust him for pardon and peace with God?

A. Yes. He is our peace.

Q. Have you not very wicked and corrupted hearts?

A. Yes. Jer. xvii. 9.

Q. Cannot

Q. Cannot you mend and change them by your own power?

A. No. Rom. v. 6.

Q. Whence then cometh your help?

A. From Jesus at the right hand of God.

Q. Can he subdue your most deep-rooted iniquities?

A. Yes. He is able to save to the uttermost.

Q. Must he reign till he hath put all enemies under his feet?

A. He must.

Q. What is the last enemy to be destroyed?

A. Death.

Q. When he hath as Mediator effected the final salvation of his people, shall he then deliver up the kingdom to the Father?

A. He shall.

Q. But will he as God-man reign with and over them for ever and ever?

A. He will. Dan. vii. 14.

Q. Well then, if this be your faith indeed, it must be influential upon your heart and conduct: if you profess to look to Jesus on the throne of glory, are you bound to submit with chearfulness to whatever he commands?

A. Certainly.

Q. But do not many call him Lord, and yet refuse to do what he commands?

A. Yes,

A. Yes, 'tis to be feared, too many.

Q. Are all the difpenfations of his providence to be fubmitted to with refignation?

A. Yes, for he doth all things well.

Q. Then to murmur or repine is rebellion againft Jefus on the throne?

A. No doubt it is.

Q. Are you bound to truft him then with all your concerns of body or foul in time or eternity?

A. I am.

Q. Can you glorify him by any means fo much as by this confident dependence on his power, care, faithfulnefs, and love?

A. By no other way, like this.

Q. And is it not a moft comfortable confideration to behold all our interefts lodged in his hands?

A. Yes, moft comfortable indeed.

Q. Then ought we not to be joyful in our King?

A. Yes, always rejoicing. Phil. iv. 4.

C. The Lord enable you to be fo. Faith in your exalted head Jefus, will bring abiding joy into the heart. A view of him at the right hand of God, will fupport you under temptation, perfecution, and affliction. Thus Stephen ftoned, faw his glory, and died triumphantly. And he is the fame yefterday, to-day, and for ever. He hath done nothing for any one of his people that you

and

and I may not confidently expect, that in a like case with theirs, if needful, he would do for us. His love is unchangeable, his power undiminished. Oh that we kept the view of our glorified Jesus more abidingly before us! Then should we undoubtedly go on conquering and to conquer, and follow him to the throne eternal in the heavens!

XVIII.

We believe that thou shalt come to judge the world, say we in the beautiful hymn called the Te Deum: and a matter of joyful confession is this to every real follower of the once crucified, but now exalted Jesus. For when he shall appear the second time it will be without sin for our salvation, and therefore we shall appear with him in glory. Prepare then, my dear children, to meet your God!

Q. Shall the Lord Jesus ever come again into this world?

A. He shall.

Q. From whence shall he come?

A. From heaven. 1 Thess. iv. 16.

Q. What will be his business when he comes?

A. To be our Judge.

Q. Whom shall he judge?

A. All mankind, the quick or living, and the dead.

Q. Will

Q. Will the eternal state of all men be determined by him?

A. It will.

Q. Is it not an awful consideration to think of appearing before our eternal Judge?

A. Very awful.

Q. How will men be judged?

A. According to their works, whether they be good, or whether they be evil.

Q. Ought not then the apprehension of giving an account to God in judgment to have a weighty influence on your temper and conduct?

A. It ought, no doubt.

Q. Shall we give an account for every secret thought, and every idle word?

A. We shall. Eccles. xii. 14.

C. How careful then should we be over our words and works, that we may find mercy with the Lord at that day?—But you dont imagine that you can justify yourselves before him by your works?

A. No. In his sight can no flesh living be justified.

Q. How then will you have boldness to stand in the day of judgment?

A. I will make mention of his righteousness only. Psal. lxxi. 16.

Q. Can

Q. Can you be presented without spot before God any other way?

A. No. If he mark what is amiss in us, who can abide it?

Q. Then you must be justified before God by faith at the day of judgment as well as this moment?

A. Yes. The just shall live by faith.

Q. Yet you say we are to be judged by our works, are these then to prove the reality of our faith?

A. They are. Jam. ii. 18.

Q. Is a true faith to be known by good works, as a living tree by its fruits?

A. It is.

Q. Though our works cannot stand in the judgment because at best poor and imperfect, yet will they follow us to witness the reality of our faith, as working by love?

A. They will. Rev. xiv. 13.

Q. Will they who by wicked works prove the hypocrisy of their profession, be found infidels in fact at that day?

A. Assuredly.

Q. Who then will be damned?

A. Those who believe not.

Q. But have not all men faith?

A. No, very few. 2 Thess. iii. 2. Matt. vii. 14.

Q. Does

Q. Does not every body in the church repeat this article of their creed?

A. They do.

Q. Then you suppose many speak these words, who never feel their power and truth?

A. Indeed I do.

C. Yes, my dear little pupils, lip profession is general, the faith of God's elect rare. Our Lord when he comes shall scarce find it upon earth. Be assured, they whose hearts and lives are not affected by the views of approaching judgment, do not really believe it. Though they may have taken up the matter as a notion, it does not influence them as a fixed principle. Hence among the multitude of nominal believers, who say they expect Jesus as their judge, you see so many living habitually under the power of those sins, concerning which he hath expresly said, that they who do such things shall not inherit the kingdom of God.

Q. When will Christ come to judge?

A. Of that day and hour knoweth no man.

Q. May it be this very day or night?

A. It may.

Q. Then ought we to be always ready?

A. Yes, surely. Luke xii. 40.

Q. Will he come in a day when men look not for him, and in an hour they are not aware of?

A. So he has told us.

Q. Will his coming be a matter of joy to his people?

A. Yes, he will come to be glorified in his saints, and to be admired of all that believe.

Q. Is this the character of his people, *believing saints?*

A. It is.

C. See then that you be found among the blessed number, if so, you will be glad to meet your Master in the clouds, and be enabled to say, come quickly, Lord Jesus. When others are crying to rocks to cover them, and hills to hide them from the presence of the Lamb, you will be lifting up your heads, knowing that your redemption draweth nigh. When the wicked shall be cast into hell, and all the nations who forget God: an abundant entrance shall be ministred to you into the everlasting kingdom of our God and Saviour Jesus Christ. Go then, my dear children, from your earliest infancy, remember Jesus the judge standeth at the door: live under the habitual impression of his coming: consider yourselves in jeopardy every hour, and therefore every hour walk, as those who are listening for the archangels trumpet. Then that sound shall not bring terror or dismay to you, but as the silver trumpet of jubilee call you up from your banishment below, to your inheritance, incorruptible,

incorruptible, undefiled, that fadeth not away, referved for you in heaven.

XIX.

Q. Which is the third perfon of the ever bleffed Trinity, in whom you profefs to believe?

A. I believe in the Holy Ghoft.

Q. Is the Holy Ghoft God?

A. Yes. He is one with the Father and the Son, in the glory of the undivided Godhead.

Q. Is this exprefsly declared in Scripture?

A. Yes. Acts v. 3, 4.

Q. Were you baptized in his name?

A. I was, equally with the Father and Son.

Q. Is he fet forth in fcripture as the object of divine adoration?

A. He is. 2 Cor. xiii. 14.

Q. What is his peculiar office in the work of redemption?

A. He fanctifieth me, and all the elect people of God.

Q. Is there nothing pure and holy but what proceeds from his divine infpirations?

A. Nothing. For from him alone all holy defires, all good counfels, and all juft works do proceed.

Q. Cannot

Q. Cannot any man do the least thing pleasing to God, unless he is led by the Spirit of God?

A. No. For they that are in the flesh cannot please God.

Q. Must we then be born of the Spirit before we can enter the kingdom of God?

A. We must, or else can never see God in glory. John iii. 3.

Q. What means doth the Holy Ghost use to quicken you to newness of life?

A. Generally the word of God, or his providences.

Q. What is his first work upon the conscience?

A. He convinces of sin. John xvi. 8.

Q. Do you never truly feel your guilt and misery till the Spirit of God quickens your conscience to sensibility?

A. No, till then I am dead in trespasses and sins. Eph. ii. 1.

Q. Must he also take the things of Christ and shew them unto you?

A. Yes, or I shall never savingly know him as my God and Saviour.

Q. Can no man then say that Jesus is the Christ but by the Spirit of God?

A. No man. 1 Cor. xii. 3.

C. True, my dear child. As far as the lip goes a man may *say* he is the Christ, but no man can make that confession with any experimental sense of his all-sufficiency to save, till the Holy Ghost hath discovered to the conscience the glory of the person of our God-man Jesus, and the perfection of his work on the behalf of poor sinners: convincing us of that everlasting righteousness, in which we must stand compleat before the throne of God. John xvi. 10.

Q. Is the Holy Ghost also, the author of all divine comfort to the sinner's conscience?

A. He is. John xiv. 16.

Q. Doth he shed abroad a sense of the love of God in our hearts?

A. He doth. Rom. v. 5.

Q. Is it his office to bear witness to his own work in the hearts of the redeemed?

A. It is. For the Spirit itself beareth witness with our spirits that we are the children of God. Rom. viii. 16.

Q. Is it any presumption then to be persuaded that we are now in God's favour?

A. No. It is the privilege of all God's people. 1 John iv. 13.

Q. You say the Holy Ghost thus sanctifies you and all the elect people of God, do you believe there is an elect or chosen people?

A. I do.

Q. Did

Q. Did God appoint any of the children of men from the beginning unto salvation?

A. He did. 2 Thess. ii. 13.

Q. Was this designation and appointment before they had done good or evil?

A. It was. He hath chosen us in Christ before the foundation of the world. Eph. i. 4.

Q. Did Christ as the Redeemer undertake expressly for as many as the Father had given him?

A. He did. John vi. 39.

Q. Are these called peculiarly his sheep?

A. They are. John x. 16.

Q. Did he die for them particularly?

A. He did. John x. 15.

Q. Is every individual man in the world chosen in Christ Jesus, and sanctified by the Holy Ghost?

A. No, certainly.

Q. How can you then know whether you belong to God's elect or not?

A. By the sanctification of the Spirit unto obedience, and the sprinkling of the blood of Jesus Christ. 1 Pet. i. 2.

Q. Does this doctrine of God's election tend to make men careless in their lives and conduct?

A. No, in no wise. He hath chosen us that we should be holy and without blame before him in love. Eph. i. 4.

C. What God then hath joined thus together, we may not put afunder.

Q. Is it an encouragement to us to ſtrive againſt ſin, and to perfect holineſs in the fear of God, that he worketh in us to will and to do of his good pleaſure?

A. Yes, the greateſt in the world.

Q. Will the preſumption of being elected, lead us to careleſſneſs and ſecurity?

A. No, ſurely, but to give all diligence to make our calling and election ſure, working out our own ſalvation with fear and trembling.

C. Certainly, my dear children, and very dark are they reſpecting God's word, who ſuppoſe the riches of God's love to his elect people, ſhould be made by them an occaſion of ſin. The truly choſen of God, are created in Chriſt Jeſus unto good works, God having before ordained that they ſhould walk in them; he hath predeſtinated them to be conformed to the image of his Son: and this is his will concerning them, even their ſanctification. 'Tis true the beſt things are liable to abuſe. Falſe profeſſors have often dared to challenge God as their God, and vaunted themſelves as his elect, whilſt their lives have given the lie to their lips. Through ſuch men the adverſaries of the Lord have taken occaſion to blaſpheme, but the foundation of God ſtandeth ſure, having this ſeal, the Lord knoweth them that are his. And if you and I. claim a part among his elect, the next sentence bids us shew it; *let every one that nameth the name of Christ, depart from iniquity.* It would be folly, yea, the heighth of presumption to fancy ourselves God's elect, if we are strangers to the power of his Spirit, and prove by our lives and tempers that we are habitually the slaves of sin and corruption. *As many as are led by the Spirit of God, they are the sons of God.* Mind this, my dear children, and remember the express words of your catechism, that if you are a true believer, the Holy Ghost *sanctifieth* you as one of the elect people of God.

XX.

C. We have been considering the great object of saving faith, the triune God. We have set forth to you the persons of the undivided Godhead, the Father, Son, and Holy Ghost, in glory equal, in majesty coeternal, and have declared to you the several offices, which each graciously sustains in the œconomy of the sinners salvation, as their Creator, Redeemer, and Sanctifier. We come now to that glorious body of which Christ is the living head, and to the transcendent privileges which he hath procured for every individual member of it.

Q. Is

Q. Is Chrift the head of his people?
A. He is. Col. i. 18.

Q. What is their general name?
A. The church. Col. i. 24

Q. Do you fuppofe the church to be the building, or the people?
A. The people. Acts xiv. 27.

Q. Does it comprehend all believers in every age. and nation?
A. It does.

Q. You do not imagine that any particular church, as the church of England, or Scotland, or Germany, is alone the true church of Chrift?
A. No. They are but different members of the catholic church.

Q. You call it therefore *catholic,* don't you, or univerfal?
A. I do.

Q. But you do not think that all who call themfelves of the church belong to it?
A. No. Many have a name to live, but are dead.

Q. Is this *catholic* church, holy?
A. Yes.

Q. Are the true members, therefore, of the catholic church called to be faints or holy?
A. Certainly. 1 Cor. i. 2.

Q. Can a person who lives in ungodliness, have a real part and interest in the holy catholic church?

A. No.

Q. But do not many call themselves Christians and churchmen, whose works prove they are of the synagogue of satan?

A. Yes, very many.

Q. If the church is *catholic*, you ought not then rashly to excommunicate or condemn those who profess faith in the same God and Saviour, though they may differ from you in modes of worship?

A. No, to be sure.

C. No, indeed we ought not. This spirit of bitterness, and narrow bigotry is utterly unbecoming a living member of Christ's holy catholic church: whether men pray with a form in public or without one, whether the minister officiates in a cloak or a surplice; whether they stand or sit at the Lord's supper, these and the like unessential differences enter not into the reality of church membership. They who hold the head Christ, are our brethren in the Lord; and they who are not vitally united to him, though they should have a name in the best constituted particular church, it will stand them in no stead, they have no part or lot in Christ Jesus, and are but as a branch dried up and withered, that hangs to the tree, but receives

ceives no nourishment from it, which men gather and cast into the fire, and it is burned.

Q. Does it shew an anti-christian spirit for any particular church to assume the name of catholic, in exclusion to all others?

A. It doth.

Q. Is this the case with the church of Rome?

A. It is.

C. That very church, whose corruptions are so desperate, and idolatry infamous, dares to assume infallibility, and to damn all who differ from her. Blessed be God we are reformed from her abominations.

Q. Do you think 'tis essential to the being of a church, that the word of God should be truly preached, and the sacraments duly ministred?

A. I do.

Q. Does the church of England particularly provide for this?

A. Yes, with all possible care.

Q. How?

A. By requiring subscription from her ministers, to the great articles of the Christian faith?

Q. Hath not every member of the church of England, a demand upon their minister, to preach conformably to the articles he hath subscribed?

A. To be sure.

Q. Are all the emoluments of the church bestowed as the reward for so doing?

A. They are.

Q. Must it then be very criminal to take the pay of the church of England under subscription to her articles, and preach contrary to them?

A. Very criminal. It is glaring hypocrisy, and scandalous and avowed fraud.

Q. If the due administration of the sacraments are essential to the being of a church, what think you of those who being of years of discretion, neglect them?

A. They shew they belong not to Christ, and have no part in his church.

Q. Suppose a person comes into the church, and instead of seriously hearing God's word preached, carelessly falls asleep, or goes away and mocks, and ridicules the word, do you think such a one a member of Christ's holy catholic church?

A. No certainly.

C. Well, my dear little ones, I pray God that you may be not in name but in deed true churchmen; that you may attend upon the ordinances, feel the power of the word preached, enjoy the comfort of the holy sacraments, and be every day growing up into him who is your head, Christ, proving that you are living members of his mystical body, by the purity of your tempers and conduct,

walking

walking as becometh saints, in all holy conversation and godliness; shewing the true catholic spirit of universal love to every brother in the same Lord, and praying that all our differences may be composed, our breaches repaired, our divisions healed, and that we may in one place, and with one mind and mouth, glorify God the Father, Son, and Spirit, rejoicing in the felicity of his chosen, and giving thanks with his inheritance.

XXI.

C. Having considered the holy catholic church as the collective body of all faithful people, we proceed to examine the blessings and privileges peculiar to every true member of it.

Q. What is the first of these?

A. The communion of saints.

Q. Are there any such persons as *saints* now upon the earth?

A. Yes.

Q. Is every member of Christ's church called to be a saint?

A. He is. Col. i. 2.

Q. Is it their relation to him which gives them a right to this title?

A. It is.

Q. People are used to think that there are no saints but those who have a red letter in the kalendar before their name, but is not every believer in Jesus as truly a saint as Peter or Paul?

A. To be sure he is.

Q. We are used to look up to the saints as beings exalted upon a pedestal, and to think that they were not men of like passions with ourselves, that they were perfect creatures, and that it would be a kind of presumption to attempt being like them; but do you suppose there was ever a saint of God upon earth without sin?

A. Certainly not. 1 Kings viii. 46.

Q. Were they compassed about with infirmity as well as we?

A. They were. Acts xiv. 15.

Q. Hath the book of God concealed the blemishes of the most eminent prophets and apostles?

A. No, in no wise.

Q. May not a man be in his own eyes a poor sinner, and yet considered as a saint in the sight of God?

A. To be sure he may; in Christ; who is our sanctification.

Q. Is every saint of God called to be a holy man in his life and conversation?

A. Certainly. As he who hath called us is holy, so should we be in all manner of conversation.

Q. But

Q. But do we not in many things all offend?

A. Assuredly we do. Jam. iii. 2.

Q. May we, notwithstanding our manifold infirmities, consider ourselves as God's saints?

A. Certainly: if we hold fast the head Christ.

Q. Can any hold communion and fellowship with the saints, who is not a saint himself?

A. No. What communion hath he that believeth with an infidel?

Q. Do the saints in heaven and earth hold communion?

A. Yes. We being many are one body, and members one of another.

Q. Are they our fellows, and companions?

A. They are.

Q. Ought you then to pray to them?

A. No. That were gross idolatry.

Q. You may, however, bless God for their good examples, and pray to be followers of their faith and patience?

A. To be sure, I ought to do so.

Q. Don't you think it is very sinful to ridicule the people of God, and give them the name of saints in derision?

A. Very sinful.

Q Are mockers regarded of God as persecutors in Scripture?

A. They are. Gal. iv. 29. Gen. xxi. 9.

Q. Ought

Q. Ought you to be ashamed of the scoffs of the wicked?

A. No, in no wise.

Q. Then, let the reproach cast on them be never so great, should you delight in the saints which are in the earth?

A. I should.

Q. Do the saints of God meet to hold sacred communion together?

A. They do?

Q. Wherein doth this communion consist?

A. In mutual love, expressed by kindness in word and deed towards each other.

Q. Do they join in prayer and praise, and at the Lord's table?

A. Yes; they thus maintain fellowship with Christ their head, and with one another.

Q. May you be sure that a person who does not pray, and praise God; neglects the table of the Lord; and the society of the saints, hath no part or lot among them?

A. Certainly. The tree is known by its fruits.

C. Remember this, and as you profess to believe a communion of saints, see that you belong to them, live in fellowship with them, walk as becometh your name and profession, and be followers of those who through faith and patience inherit the promises: you will then shortly join them, and

from

from a suffering saint in the church militant upon earth, become a glorified saint in the church triumphant in heaven.

XXII.

Q. What is the second privilege peculiar to the members of the holy catholic church?

A. The forgiveness of sin.

Q. Are you a sinner?

A. I am.

Q. Were you born in sin?

A. Yes.

Q. And have you committed actual sin in thought, word, and deed, times innumerable?

A. I have.

Q. Are you a great sinner, greater than you can express?

A. I am. For who can understand his errors? Psal. xix. 12.

Q. What is the wages of sin?

A. Death spiritual, temporal, and eternal.

Q. Must you suffer this as a sinner?

A. Undoubtedly I must, if my sins are not forgiven.

Q. Cannot you do any thing to procure your pardon?

A. No.

A. No. I am utterly helpless, and weak as I am wicked. Rom. v. 6.

Q. If you are sorry for your sins, will not that avail?

A. No. For sorrow pays no debts.

Q. If you resolve to do better, will not that gain your pardon?

A. No. Because if I do all that I am commanded, I do no more than is my present duty, and that cannot compensate for past transgressions.

Q. Don't you think many trust to what they call their repentance, to a little sorrow, and a hasty resolution?

A. I am afraid they do.

Q. Is it exceedingly dangerous to the soul, to be mistaken in this matter?

A. No doubt it is.

Q. Must we despair of any power in ourselves to help ourselves?

A. We must, or perish.

Q. Who is Christ come to save?

A. The lost and desperate. Luke xix. 10.

Q. Is it a desireable thing to feel and know this to be our true condition?

A. Most desireable.

Q. Is a true conviction of our state, as helpless sinners, the way to relief from our sins?

A. Yes.

A. Yes. Christ invites all that are weary and heavy laden to his rest. Matt. xi. 28.

Q. Is all our hope of pardon and forgiveness, grounded entirely upon the free mercy of God in Christ Jesus?

A. We can have no other scriptural hope.

Q. Has Christ undertaken, as the friend of sinners, to pay a full ransom for them?

A. He hath. 1 Tim. ii. 6.

Q. Was this ransom paid on the cross and accepted?

A. It was. He was delivered for our offences, and raised again for our justification.

Q. Is God now righteous and just to forgive the sins of every believer in Jesus?

A. His truth and justice engage him so to do.

Q. Is the blood of Christ once shed on the cross, sufficient to cleanse from all sin?

A. It is. 1 John i. 7.

Q. Is it as easy for him to save from many sins, as from few?

A. No doubt it is: for he is a Saviour to the uttermost. Heb. vii. 25.

Q. Do sinners perish because of their iniquities merely?

A. No, but because of their unbelief. They will not come to Christ that they might have life.

Q. Is

Q. Is every one who pleads by faith the blood of Christ, entitled to the pardon of sin?

A. He is. Acts xiii. 39.

Q. How can we be sure of this?

A. We have God's word, yea, his oath, to engage our confidence. Heb. vi. 18.

Q. May any man know that his sins are forgiven?

A. Yes, surely, so St. John saith. 1 John ii. 12.

Q. Is it presumption to say, my sins are forgiven?

A. No certainly. It cannot be presumption to believe that God will be true to his own promises.

Q. Nay, is it sinful to doubt it?

A. Surely it is.

Q. What do you think of those who revile, as proud and presumptuous, those who believe their sins are pardoned?

A. I think they don't believe the creed which they so often repeat.

Q. If our sins are pardoned, then there remains no condemnation?

A. No. None to them who are in Christ Jesus.

Q. Is it not a very comfortable thing, in the prospect of death and judgment, to know that we are already justified from all charges, and free from every accusation?

A. Yes,

A. Yes, surely; the greatest comfort any sinner can enjoy under the sun.

C. I pray God this may be your blessed portion. It will be, if you receive the record which God hath given of his Son, be truly incorporated into the holy catholic church, and become a lively member of the same. Many call themselves believers and churchmen, who never knew ought of the felicity of God's chosen, content themselves with a name to live, whilst they are dead, and make a profession of believing, when in fact utter strangers to the faith of God's elect, and to all gracious effects of it. But I hope better things of you. Remember your own declarations: you confess here, that God in Christ is your reconciled God, having forgiven you all your trespasses, and therefore you have hope in your death, and boldness at the day of judgment. If sin is pardoned, all must be well. May you truly believe this, live in the comfort, and die in the triumph of the forgiveness of sin.

XXIII.

Q. What is the third privilege peculiar to the members of the holy catholic church?
A. The resurrection of the body.
Q. Will men rise again with the same bodies?
A. They will.

Q. Will the qualities of the resurrection-body be different from the present?

A. Yes. This corruptible must put on incorruption, this mortal immortality, and this natural body become spiritual.

Q. How will this great change be effected?

A. By the power of Christ. The trumpet shall sound, and the dead shall be raised, and those who are alive, be changed in a moment.

Q. What will follow the resurrection?

A. The judgment.

Q. Must every man then give an account of the things he hath done in the body, according to that he hath done, whether it be good, or whether it be evil?

A. They must.

Q. But if all men rise again, what is the privilege of Christ's people above others?

A. They shall rise first — and their bodies be fashioned like to Christ's glorious body. 1 Thess. iv. 16. Phil. iii. 21.

Q. What will be the case of the ungodly and the sinner?

A. They will awake to shame, and everlasting contempt.

Q. Is the consideration of a glorious resurrection, a strong support against the fears of death?

A. A very strong one.

Q. Will

Q. Will not the change be unspeakably to our advantage?

A. Yes. When our earthly house of this tabernacle is dissolved, we have a building of God, a house not made with hands, eternal in the heavens.

Q. Should this reconcile us to part with our dearest friends and relatives in the Lord?

A. It should. For we sorrow not as those who have no hope.

Q. Shall we certainly meet again?

A. Yes, assuredly, we shall go to them, though they cannot return to us.

Q. Will it be a joyful meeting?

A. Yes; never to part again.

Q. Shall we know each other in that day?

A. It seems so. Dives knew Lazarus, and we are told of seeing Abraham, Isaac, and Jacob, in the kingdom.

C. Prepare then for this great change. Live as expecting the archangel's trumpet, and be more careful to secure a glorious resurrection body, than about this wretched clod, and the meat which perisheth; then whenever your summons comes you will welcome it, and springing from the dust, will lift up your heads with transport, and triumph in the great day of the Lord, knowing your redemption draweth nigh, and being caught up to meet him in the air, you will thenceforth forever be with the

the Lord. Comfort your hearts therefore with these words.

XXIV.

C. We are now come to the last article of our creed, that consummation so devoutly wished for by every redeemed sinner, when he shall enter into the rest that remaineth for the people of God, and be in possession of that joy and felicity both in body and soul, in Christ's kingdom of eternal glory, which is as inconceivable, as it will be enduring. Tell me then, what is the last privilege peculiar to members of the holy catholic church?

A. Life everlasting.

Q. Will death itself be then destroyed?

A. Yes. The last enemy which shall be destroyed is death.

Q. Where will the abode of God's people be?

A. In heaven.

Q. What will be their blessedness there?

A. The fruition of his glorious Godhead.

Q. Will they be like him?

A. Yes. They will awake up in his perfect image, and be as happy as he can make them.

Q. What will be their employment?

A. To love and praise, like the angels.

Q. Who will be their companions?

A. All

A. All the heavenly host.

Q. Is the glory of heaven beyond all our present conceptions?

A. Yes. Eye hath not seen, nor ear heard, neither hath it entered into the heart of man, what good things God hath prepared for those that love him.

Q. Is their state described as of transcendent dignity?

A. It is, in the highest terms—they have crowns of gold upon their heads—conquering palms in their hands—robes of righteousness to cover them, and thrones of glory—yea, they shall sit down with Christ on his throne, as he is sat down with the Father on his throne.

Q. What will become of the impenitent and unbelieving?

A. They will be driven from Christ's judgment seat, into everlasting fire, with the devil and his angels.

Q. Why do you say, amen, at the end of the creed?

A. Because I express thereby, both my confidence in these truths, and my prayer that these privileges may be mine.

Q. And do you hope they will be yours?

A. So I trust, through the mercy of my God in Jesus Christ.

C. Hold

C. Hold fast then this hope of eternal life, which God, who cannot lie, hath promised before the world began. He is faithful, and they that have grace to trust him, will not be disappointed of their hope. The conflict is short,—the crown is in view,—the victory sure,—fight therefore the good fight of faith, that you may lay hold on eternal life. Yet a little while and Christ, who is our life, shall appear, and then shall we appear with him in glory, and live and reign with him for ever and ever. Amen.

XXV.

C. We have at large examined the several articles of the creed, which contain the true confession of faith of God's elect. This was the second thing engaged for by our godfathers and godmothers at our baptism, that we should believe them, and what did they promise and vow thirdly in your name?

A. That I should keep God's holy will and commandments, and walk in the same all the days of my life.

Q. Where do you find God's holy will and commandments particularly revealed to you?

A. In the 20th chapter of Exodus.

Q. Did God deliver them to Moses on mount Sinai, written upon two tables of stone?

A. He

A. He did.

Q. How many commandments were there written?

A. Ten.

Q. Do these ten commandments contain the whole of what is called the *moral law?*

A. They do.

Q. Is perfection of obedience required by the law of God?

A. It is.

Q. Is there a curse denounced upon every man, that continueth not in all the things written in the book of the law, to do them?

A. There is. Deut. xxvii. 26.

Q. Have you kept all God's commandments?

A. No. I have broken them all.

Q. Then you cannot be justified before God, on account of your disobedience?

A. No. By the deeds of the law shall no flesh living be justified.

Q. Is the law holy, just, and good, notwithstanding it condemns you?

A. Yes surely. The Lord is righteous, and we are sinners.

Q. If the law is broken by you, and must condemn you for past transgression, can you at present keep it in perfection?

A. No.

A. No. In many things we all offend, and if we say we have no sin, we deceive ourselves, and the truth is not in us.

Q. Wherefore then serveth the law, if obedience to it cannot justify you before God, hath it any other ends?

A. Yes, many and great.

Q. Can you tell me what?

A. 1st. By the law is the knowledge of sin.

Q. Is this necessary that you should be brought to a sight and sense of your sins?

A. Yes, for the whole need not the physician, but those who are sick.

Q. How doth the law give the knowledge of sin?

A. By holding up the perfection it requires, and shewing me how short I come of the glory of God.

Q. What other end hath it?

A. 2dly. It is a schoolmaster to bring us to Christ, that we might be justified by faith.

Q. Doth the curse it denounces drive the sinner who feels it, to fly for refuge to the grace of the gospel?

A. It doth.

Q. Then it cannot be a covenant of life to you?

A. No. It is called the ministration of death. 2 Cor. iii. 7.

Q. But

Q. But if you are now justified by faith in Christ, is the law abolished, and doth it cease to bind the conscience?

A. No, in no wise. Though it is no longer a covenant of life, it remains a rule of duty.

Q. Do we then by faith make void the law?

A. God forbid. Yea, we establish the law.

Q. What is the sum and substance of the moral law?

A. Love to God and our neighbour?

Q. Hath faith any influence upon the conscience to produce this love?

A. Yes, the strongest imaginable.

Q. Doth God sanctify his people through the power of faith?

A. He doth, as we are told. Acts xv. 9.

Q. When you promise therefore obedience to God's holy will and commandments, you do it, as a believer in Jesus?

A. I do.

Q. Must all your services be accepted for, and in him?

A. They must. We are accepted in the beloved, and our services are well pleasing to God, through Jesus Christ.

Q. Can you do any service acceptable to God, but as you live by faith?

A. None.

A. None. For without faith it is impossible to please God.

Q. Hath the doctrine of faith then an unfavourable influence upon morality?

A. Just the very reverse. It worketh by love. And this is the love of God, that we keep his commandments, and his commandments are not grievous.

Q. Do you imagine that they who oppose the doctrines of faith and grace, are real enemies to true holiness?

A. Assuredly. For they oppose that which only can purify the heart, and that God requires in the first place.

Q. As a believer in Jesus, do you purpose to follow his holy mind and will, as far as it is revealed to you?

A. I do.

Q. But have you strength to accomplish your holy purposes?

A. Not in my-self. In me, that is, in my flesh, dwelleth no good thing.

Q. Whence cometh your help?

A. From Christ alone, whose strength is made perfect in my weakness.

Q. How do you draw out of his fulness?

A. By the prayer of faith.

Q. Are

Q. Are you then created of God in Christ Jesus unto good works, God having before ordained that you should walk in them?

A. As a believer, I am.

Q. And must you henceforth live for him who died for you?

A. The love of Christ constraineth me to judge that I ought to do so.

C. May the Lord enable you with his grace for all the good pleasure of his will, and work in you the work of faith with power; adorn the doctrine of God your Saviour in all things, and let your light so shine before men that they may see your good works, and glorify your Father which is in heaven. True faith ever wrought the most powerful change on the heart and temper, and the blood of Christ sprinkled there infallibly purges the conscience from dead works to serve the living God.

XXVI.

C. The commandments of God, though no longer a covenant of life, are the rule of moral duty; and whilst as a school-master they lead us to Christ that we might be justified by faith, they point out the path in which under the influence of faith working by love, we are called to walk as children of God.

Q. What do you chiefly learn by the commandments?

A. I learn two things, my duty towards God, and my duty towards my neighbour.

Q. What is your duty towards God?

A. My duty towards God, is to believe in him, to fear him, and to love him with all my heart, with all my mind, with all my soul, and with all my strength; to worship him, to give him thanks, to put my whole trust in him, to call upon him, to honour his holy name, and his word, and to serve him truly all the days of my life.

Q. This is the substance of the first four commandments. What is the first commandment?

A. Thou shalt have none other Gods but me.

Q. Is there any other God, but the Lord?

A. There is no other.

Q. But have not men set up many false Gods?

A. They have.

Q. How is the true God to be known?

A. From the revelation he hath made of himself in the Scriptures.

Q. Must our acquaintance with God be derived from the Bible, before we can worship, serve and obey him as we ought to do?

A. It must.

Q. What is chiefly required by this commandment?

A. That

A. That I should believe in him.

Q. Is all our knowledge of the true God matter of faith?

A. It is.

Q. Do you suppose that human reason without a revelation from God, would ever have led us to know God?

A. No. In no wise. 1 Cor. i. 21.

Q. What should your knowledge of God and faith in him lead you to in the first place?

Q. To fear him.

Q. Must you fear offending him as the greatest of all evils?

A. I ought to do so.

Q. Should no fear of any creature ever sway or influence you to act contrary to his will?

A. No in no wise.

Q. Suppose you were threatened to be burnt at a stake for your duty towards God, ought you to lay down your life rather than sin against him?

A. Yes, assuredly.

Q. Why must you thus fear him?

A. Because all others can only destroy the body, but he can cast both soul and body into hell.

Q. Ought you to fear offending not merely as a slave through fear, but as a child?

A. Certainly. If I were not punished for it, I should fear the very offence.

Q. Should

Q. Should you love God as well as fear him?

A. Certainly.

Q. How much.

A. With all my heart, and mind, and soul, and strength.

Q. Ought you to love nothing in comparison with him?

A. No. Nothing in comparison with him. Pſal. lxxiii. 25.

Q. Does this commandment enjoin you to worſhip him?

A. It doth.

Q. What worſhip doth God require, inward or outward?

A. Both.

Q. Doth he demand our hearts?

A. He doth.

Q. Will it ſignify any thing to give him the lip and the knee if the heart be far from him?

A. It will not. Matt. xv. 8.

Q. Will the pretended prayers of thoſe who draw near to him with their lips whilſt their heart is far from him condemn them?

A. They will. Their very prayers are turned into ſin.

Q. Are you alſo hereby engaged to thank God continually?

A. I am.

Q. Are

Q. Are you receiving many blessings from him?

A. Yes, very many.

Q. Should you not therefore acknowledge it to his glory?

A. That is my bounden duty.

Q. Must you put your whole trust in him?

A. I should do so.

Q. Must you depend upon him for all your concerns of body and soul, in time and to eternity?

A. Yes, for all.

Q. Do you think you have always thus feared, loved, worshipped, and trusted in God with all your heart?

A. No. In many things we all offend.

Q. How will you then at present gain peace in your conscience?

A. Through faith in Jesus Christ. Rom. v. 1.

Q. Is he the end of the law for righteousness to every one that believeth?

A. He is.

Q. Should it not humble you before God, when you see how short you come of his holy law?

A. It ought so to do.

Q. And should it stir you up to call upon him for grace, and strength to cleave to him more faithfully?

A. Certainly it should.

Q. Do

Q. Do you think there are at present any idolaters?

A. Yes, very many.

Q. Who are they?

A. All who love, fear, and trust in any creature more than the living God.

C. True, my dear child. Take care, therefore, that the case be not your own. If you have taken the Lord for your God, let none rival him in your hearts. Set him always before you. Live in the sense of his presence. Believe he sees, hears and notices all that passes. Fear, therefore, to sin against him. Love him unfeignedly, sensible of his infinite grace to you, and your infinite obligations. Love him above all things, delighting in him as your portion, and desiring conformity to his image, as your greatest felicity. Trust him, in sickness, in health, in poverty, in distress, in every trial, in every affliction, whether of body or soul: and never cease crying to him from the heart, that he will be your God, and manifest himself unto you as he doth not unto the world; then, though you cannot endure the severity of his judgment, you shall enjoy the experience of his grace in Christ, in pardoning what is amiss, strengthening what is weak, and perfecting that which is lacking: According to his own sure word of promise, I will be their God, and they shall be my people, and I will put my laws into their hearts, and in their minds will I write them, and their sins and iniquities will I remember no more.

XXVII.

C. The first commandment enjoined the worship of the true God, the second directs the acceptable manner of worshipping him; for we are not allowed to follow our own will and fancy, but must attend to his revealed word, what is the second commandment?

A. Thou shalt not make to thyself any graven image, nor the likeness of any thing that is in heaven above, or in the earth beneath, or in the water under the earth. Thou shalt not bow down to them, nor worship them: for I the Lord thy God am a jealous God, and visit the sins of the fathers upon the children, unto the third and fourth generation of them that hate me; and shew mercy unto thousands in them that love me, and keep my commandments.

Q. What does this commandment forbid?

A. All image worship.

Q. Are the papists therefore guilty of idolatry, when they worship the images of our Lord, his cross, and the figures of dead men?

A. Yes, of gross idolatry.

Q. Is it possible to form any real resemblance to the Godhead?

A. No.

Q. Why?

A. Because God is a Spirit.

Q. How must he then be worshipped?

A. In spirit and in truth.

Q. May we form no bodily representation of him even in our minds?

A. No.

Q. In what way are we to express our worship of God?

A. I am to call upon him,— to give him thanks — to hear, read and meditate upon his holy word — and to be found in the use of his sacraments, and all his instituted ordinances.

C. You answer very rightly. Is prayer the duty of every reasonable creature?

A. It is.

Q. Must we therefore conclude that all who live without prayer live without God in the world?

A. Assuredly.

Q. Is every prayerless person a practical atheist?

A. Undoubtedly he is.

Q. What is the nature of true prayer?

A. Prayer is the desire of the soul after God, and his mercies, proceeding from a sense of our necessities, and resting on the truth of his promises.

C. Very

C. Very well. Then you see there can be no real prayer, without these three things. 1. A sense of our necessities. 2. Faith in the promises of God through Christ that he will hear, and help us. 3. A heart-felt desire of relief, that urges us to diligence and importunity in waiting upon God.

Q. Will no form of words make a prayer if the heart be not thus affected?

A. Certainly not.

Q. Do you not therefore think that many deceive themselves in this matter, who suppose they have said their prayers when they have read so many words out of a book?

A. I am afraid they do.

C. And so am I too. Many there are who go on in formality reading their prayers, morning and evening, and call this praying, who perhaps have used the same book, and the same words for years, and years together, without ever thinking whether they felt, what they said, or expected an answer to their petitions, supposing the work is done merely, when they have come to the Amen. This is gross self-delusion, and hypocrisy, and such formal unmeaning services, can only bring a curse instead of a blessing upon the soul. If we read a volume of prayers every day, and knelt till our knees were as hard as a camel's, if our conscience was not affected; our heart sensible, our faith in exercise and real defire after God, dictated our words, all our reading would be but as founding brass or tinkling cymbal, and not a word of real prayer be found in ten thousand million of such formal acts of devotion.

Q. Is a composed form of words necessary in order to prayer?

A. No.

Q. Ought every man to pray as he feels his heart affected, even as the hungry beggar asks an alms?

A. To be sure, this is most natural.

Q. You don't think we are heard for our fine speaking, or much speaking?

A. No certainly.

Q. Do you suppose a composed form of words *unlawful?*

A. No. Not if they express what I really feel.

C. So I apprehend, and as to the *expedience*, every man must be the best judge for himself. In public worship, it is my own opinion, that *a form of sound words* is preferable to free prayer in general; in private, though I would not refuse any useful assistance, nor prescribe invariable rules, I should prefer speaking the present feelings of the heart as they arise, less curious about the expression, and more solicitous about the matter.

Q. Are

Q. Are you to thank and praise God for the blessings you receive, as well as pray to him for the mercies you need?

A. That is my bounden duty.

Q. How are you to express your thanks?

A. With my lips, and in my life.

Q. How do you express your thanks in your lips?

A. In prayer acknowledging the mercies of the Lord: and speaking in psalms and hymns and spiritual songs, singing and making melody in the heart unto the Lord?

Q. Is psalm and hymn singing a part of God's worship?

A. It is.

Q. What think you of those who ridicule these things?

A. That they are profane, and despisers of God and godliness.

Q. How are you to express your thankfulness in your life?

A. By glorifying God in my body and in my spirit which are his.

Q. What is your duty with regard to the word of God?

A. To read, mark, learn, and inwardly digest it.

Q. Were

Q. Were not your godfathers and godmothers at your baptism charged that they should call upon you to hear sermons?

A. Yes they were.

Q. Are you bound therefore to a conscientious attendance upon the ministry of God's word?

A. I am.

Q. Should you search the Scriptures diligently, to prove all things, and hold fast that which is good?

A. I should do so.

Q. You are not to take your minister's word therefore, nor any other persons, without examining for yourselves, ought you?

A. No.

Q. Is it a part of your duty towards God, to enquire out of his own word what is his holy will?

A. Assuredly it is.

Q. Do you suppose they can have any regard for God or their souls, who never open their bibles for weeks and months together?

A. To be sure, they seem to have none.

Q. How should you search the Scriptures in order to know God's mind and will?

A. 1. Humbly, sensible of my spiritual ignorance. 2. Diligently, as knowing it of the last importance to my salvation that I, hold the truth. 3. With prayer for divine illumination.

C. True,

C. True, my dear child, and the meek will he teach his ways. In this method of seeking after God, he will instruct you, and make you wise unto salvation. Of the sacraments I shall speak to you in another place, reserving what I have to say till then; I shall only add to what I have remarked above, that when we reflect upon the coldness, deadness, and hypocrisy of our prayers, the formality of our devotion, the languor of our praises, the neglect of God's word, our inattention to, and unprofitableness under it, we have much reason to feel our consciences condemned, and to cry, as we are taught to do after every commandment is read, Lord have mercy upon us. For under no one of them, can we stand justified by our obedience.

Q. Is God jealous of his honour and glory?

A. Yes. He is a jealous God, visiting the iniquities of the fathers upon their children, unto the third and fourth generation of them that hate him, and shewing mercy unto thousands in them that love him, and keep his commandments.

Q. It is a dreadful thing to hate God, is it not?

A. Yes. Truly diabolical.

Q. But do not those who neglect God, restrain prayer, and cast his word behind their backs, express therein their hatred to him?

A. No.

A. No doubt they do; for their conduct faith moſt ſtrongly, depart from us, for we deſire not the knowledge of thy ways.

Q. How does God viſit the iniquities of the fathers upon the children?

A. The children ſuffer in conſequence of the temporal miſeries, which their ungodly parents bring upon themſelves.

Q. Is it a great bleſſing to have godly parents?

A. Yes. God ſheweth mercy unto thouſands in them that love him, and keep his commandments?

C. You ſee, therefore, the beſt patrimony a parent can leave you, is the favour of his good example, and the moſt valuable portion the bleſſing of God promiſed to the deſcendants of thoſe who love him and keep his commandments. You may, perhaps, of this world have very little to leave behind you; be it therefore the more your care to tranſmit to poſterity the mercy herein promiſed, and that will be better for them than thouſands of gold and ſilver.

XXVIII.

Q. What is the third commandment?

A. Thou ſhalt not take the name of the Lord thy

thy God in vain; for the Lord will not hold him guiltless, that taketh his name in vain.

Q. What does this commandment enjoin?

A. A reverent mention of the holy name of God, and of whatever belongs to him.

Q. Does this commandment forbid all profane cursing and swearing?

A. It doth.

Q. What think you of those, who, in their common conversation, make use of the name of God, Jesus, Christ; and cry without thinking, good God, Lord have mercy upon me, and the like?

A. They transgress grievously against this commandment.

Q. Is it not shocking to hear the name of God so blasphemed?

A. It is.

C. Indeed it is, my dear children; and women as well as men almost universally fall into this shocking profaneness. If their oaths are not such horrid imprecations as fill the mouths of male blasphemers, they make perhaps a more frequent, light, wanton, and irreverent use of the name of the Most High, than even men do, as I have often observed; and from the excessive frequency of doing it, are even insensible of what they say, and when reproved, I have, by experience, known them

them deny they did it, when the very next sentence repeated the transgression. Never take this holy name in your mouth. A child of God never hears it done, but it grieves him.

Q. Is great guilt brought upon the conscience, by the light and wanton use of God's name?

A. Assuredly. God will not hold him guiltless who taketh his name in vain.

Q. Can people take God's name in vain in their prayers?

A. Yes; when they pretend to speak to God, without a reverential sense of his presence on their hearts.

Q. Is God's *word* to be made use of with respect?

A. Yes.

Q. What think you of those who turn it into ridicule,—jest upon it,—and in their common talk, or, perhaps over their cups indecently, and irreverently, quote the word of God?

A. Such despisers of God's word, will one day shortly, wonder and perish.

Q. Is God provoked when his people are treated ill?

A. He is greatly. He that toucheth them, toucheth the apple of his eye.

C. Yet

C. Yet the world is even ready to brand their profession as hypocrisy—to blazon their failings—and malign their graces—to give an invidious turn to whatever can be misrepresented—and always to have their ears open to hear, and their hearts open to believe every railing accusation brought against them.

Q. Is it very criminal to be thus despisers and revilers of those that are good?

A. Very criminal. What is done to the least of his people, God will regard as done against himself.

Q. May we not by our conduct dishonour God's name?

A. Yes, highly: if by any evil thing, we give occasion to the adversaries of the Lord to blaspheme: as David did.

Q. Are we bound in our conversation with each other, to set forth God's glory?

A. This should be our desire.

Q. Should we speak good of God's name?

A. This is the best use of our tongues, to be employed to his glory, and for the good of men's souls.

C. Yes, my dear children, it is so. But when prophaneness is so triumphant, to open our mouths with a view to glorify God's holy name, is looked upon as some strange thing. A word dropt of serious

rious conversation, makes often a dead pause, in company; and the gentlest reproof of those, who take God's name in vain, is thought rudeness and ill-manners. You must be content to be unlike the world, therefore, if you would not be condemned with it. And in this one particular, among others, the difference must appear, that living under an abiding sense of his presence on your heart, you never, but with awful reverence, make mention of that high and holy name, the Lord thy God.

XXIX.

Q. What is the fourth commandment?

A. Remember that thou keep holy the sabbath day. Six days shalt thou labour, and do all that thou hast to do; but the seventh day is the sabbath of the Lord thy God; in it thou shalt do no manner of work, thou, and thy son, and thy daughter, thy man-servant, and thy maid-servant, thy cattle, and the stranger that is within thy gates; for in six days the Lord made heaven and earth, the sea, and all that in them is, and rested the seventh day; wherefore the Lord blessed the seventh day, and hallowed it.

C. We are called upon every day to glorify God, and no one should pass over us, without acts of

worship

worship to him in whom we live, and move, and have our being; but one day out of seven is peculiarly and wholly appropriated for this blessed end and purpose, that abstracted from all worldly concerns, we might be wholly employed in spiritual matters, remembering the great works of creation, and redemption, and in all holy exercises preparing for the work of an eternal sabbath, when we shall rest from all our labours, and serve God day and night in his temple and go out no more.

Q. Is the day of rest which we observe, different from the jewish sabbath?

A. It is.

Q. What day do we observe?

A. The first day of the week.

Q. Why is this change?

A. To commemorate our Lord's resurrection.

Q. Was this the apostolic practice?

A. It was. John xx. 19. Acts xx. 7. 1 Cor. xvi. 2.

Q. What is required in order to the sanctification of the Lord's Day?

A. 1. A rest from all ordinary business. 2. An employment of our time in the exercises of religion to the glory of God, and the edification of our souls.

Q. May no work be done on the sabbath day?

A. Works

A. Works of neceffity, mercy, and charity are always excepted.

Q. True, if our ox fall into a pit on the fabbath day, we may draw him out. The fick, infirm, and infants, are to be attended. And fome employments can admit of no interruption without the moft hurtful confequences. In thefe cafes the fabbath was made for man, not man for the fabbath: but thefe few exceptions affect not the general fcope of the commandment.

Q. Our ordinary bufinefs then, you fay, muft be wholly laid afide.

A. It muft.

Q. May we not think about it, or talk about it?

A. No furely. Worldly thoughts and contrivances, are as much a breach of the fabbath, as any outward labours.

Q. May we not buy or fell on the Lord's day?

A. No, in no wife.

Q. How fhould we then employ our time on this day?

A. In religious exercifes, and heavenly difcourfes, and meditations.

Q. Should we ferioufly attend the public worfhip?

A. Yes. Early in our places—collected not wandering in prayer—attentive to the word preached ed—and seriously examining our consciences thereby.

Q. Should you in the evening as well as morning, be in the house of God?

A. Yes, surely.

Q. May you not take your pleasure in the evening, in idle visiting, and common discourse?

A. No. The whole day is to be employed in God's service.

C. True, my dear children. It is the Lord's day, and we rob God when we employ any of the hours contrary to the design and institution of his sacred rest. They who have families, should begin and end it with prayer and praise — catechising their servants and children — enquiring what they heard at church — examining their progress in religious knowledge — and further instructing them. They who have none, should be employed in private prayer and meditation on what they read, or hear from God's word — in religious conversation among friends, building up each other in our most holy faith — and all in their several stations, keeping in view the great end of the sabbatical rest, even to prepare for the great change, and be ready for the eternal rest which remaineth for the people of God.

Q. What think you of those, who make the sabbath a day of diversion, and idleness; riding out, and

and making parties of pleasure—what of those who are glad of any excuse, to absent themselves from the house of God—what of those who having spent the morning at their glass, instead of upon their knees, go to church to be admired, and gazed at; laughing perhaps, talking, bowing, and more attentive to each other, than to that God, whom they pretend to worship? What think you of these, do they hallow the sabbath?

A. No. They are profane sabbath breakers.

Q. Is the sabbath a burden to a child of God?

A. No. It is his delight.

Q. Does he take pleasure in the holy ordinances?

A. He doth. As David says, I was glad when they said unto me, we will go into the house of the Lord—and again, it is good for me to draw nigh unto God.

Q. Is it a bad sign when people seem weary of the sabbath day, and wish it over?

A. A very bad one.

Q. If they are weary of serving God a few hours, what would they do in heaven, where the sabbath is eternal?

A. They can have no part nor lot there.

Q. Are we bound, as far as our power or influence reaches, that others should keep holy the sabbath day as well as we?

A. Cer-

A. Certainly; even to our man-servant and maid-servant, and the stranger within our gates.

Q. Should every head of a family, therefore, contrive that those under his roof, may have all possible opportunity of attending the worship of God?

A. To be sure, they should.

C. The servant on the Lord's day, should be free as his master: and every godly master will endeavour he shall be so. We must not detain those to serve tables, who should be serving God in his house. Many make the sabbath a feast day; and think more then of good eating and drinking, than on any day of the week: their servants must be toiling for their dinners, when they should be receiving the bread of life under the word; whilst their masters, fed to the full, sleep at home, or perhaps at church, the afternoon. I lay it down as a certain truth, that they can have little regard for their servants souls, or the sanctification of the sabbath, who cannot, on that day, be content with a slight repast, not to detain them at home; besides that, as it is proved by experience, how much a hearty meal often disposes to sleep and stupefies, they who have a real delight in approaching to God, will be careful, by peculiar temperance, on that day to avoid whatever might dull their attention, and indispose them for an enlivened enjoyment

ment of the public and private worship of God. Some may, perhaps, think these observations too minute; but it is in these little things, if you will call them so, that a real concern for the sanctification of the sabbath, especially appears, and the effects of attending to these remarks, will be found, I am persuaded, of real, yea, of eternal importance.

XXX.

C. The fifth commandment is of the most extensive nature, taking in the vast circle of relative duties of every kind; and in the conscientious attention to the discharge of them, the power of vital godliness appears in the most striking and convincing manner. The most flaming profession abroad, and the most zealous labours to propagate the gospel, are evidences comparatively small of the truth of our Christianity, when compared with the spirit and temper which we manifest among those who are nearest to us, and constant observers of our conduct at home. There no disguise conceals the hypocrite, but what we really are, we shall appear, and a blessed testimony will it be to the reality of our profession, if they who are nearest and most intimately conversant with us, behold us habitually under the influence of the commandments of the Lord,

Lord, and walking worthy our high vocation and calling. To be a good parent, an obedient child; a tender husband, a faithful and gentle wife; a kind master, a diligent servant, and the like, manifests more surely that we are of God, than if we gave all our goods to feed the poor, and our bodies to be burned.

Q. What is the fifth commandment?

A. Honour thy father and thy mother, that thy days may be long in the land which the Lord thy God giveth thee.

Q. Is this commandment confined only to our parents?

A. No. It extends to all superiors.

Q. Does it not comprehend also reciprocally, the duty which all parents owe their children, and superiors their inferiors?

A. It doth.

Q. Are our obligations to each other, therefore, mutual?

A. They are.

Q. What is the first great mutual relation?

A. Between parents and children.

Q. What is the parent's duty towards their children?

A. 1. To set before them a good example.

2. To teach them the knowledge of God's revealed mind and will in his word.

3. To encourage them when they behave well.

4. To be gentle towards them; always distinguishing between their childish follies, and criminal conduct.

5. To correct them, faithfully, in measure, never in anger, and to inform them of the cause and necessity of such correction.

6. To provide for them, and take care to dispose of them in the world, so as that they may be enabled to provide for themselves.

7. To advise, though not constrain them in the article of marriage.

8. To pray with them, and for them.

Q. Do not many parents hurt their children by foolish fondness, and sinful indulgence?

A. I am afraid they do.

Q. What is the duty of children towards their parents?

A. 1. To honour their persons, as being of God most immediately entrusted with the care of their childrens bodies and souls, and all the concerns of both.

2. To obey all their lawful commands with chearfulness, and diligence.

3. To receive with thankfulness, and attention all their instructions.

4. To submit with all humility to their reproofs, or corrections, sorry for having offended, and more
troubled

troubled for the fault, than hurt by the chastisement.

5. To be content and satisfied with their disposal of them in life, persuaded that they are better judges than their children.

6. To bear with their infirmities.

7. To provide for them if necessitous.

8. To contribute in every way to their comfort, and advantage, endeavouring to requite them for all their past kind care.

Q. Does the commandment enjoin an equal honour to the mother as well as the father?

A. Yes, assuredly.

Q. Is all irreverence therefore, disobedience, inattention, murmuring, undutifulness, and the like, to either parent very sinful in the sight of God?

A. No doubt it is.

Q. Can they be God's children who show such a temper and conduct towards their parents?

A. No. In no wise.

Q. What is the next great relative duty?

A. Between husbands and wives.

Q. Is marriage a divine institution, and honourable among all?

A. It is.

Q. What is the mutual duty which husbands and wives owe each other?

A. 1. To

A. 1. To consider each other as no longer two but one flesh.

2. To have the salvation of each other's souls first in their view.

3. To study mutually how to please and render each other's life most comfortable.

4. To share each other's comforts, and to support each other's crosses.

5. To bear with each other's infirmities and faults, remembering that a corrupted creature must not expect perfection in his fellow.

6. To consult together in all matters of moment, respecting their affairs or children's good.

7. To be faithful to each other in affection, and never defile the purity of their mind or bodies, by any desire, or act contrary to the near and holy relation in which they stand.

Q. But are there not some duties annexed more peculiarly to each party severally?

A. There are.

Q. What is required of the husband particularly?

A. 1. To love their wives.

2. To give them honour.

3. Not to be bitter against them.

4. To provide for them things honest in the sight of all men.

5. To rule well their own houses.

Q. What

Q. What is especially the wife's duty?

A. 1. To reverence their husbands.

2. To be obedient in all things.

3. To be keepers at home.

4. To manage the interior of the family with diligence, œconomy, and discretion.

5. To cultivate above all things the ornament of a meek and quiet spirit, which is in God's sight of great price.

Q. What think you is the cause of such unhappiness as is often found in the marriage state?

A. Because the most meet together merely as brute beasts, to satisfy their carnal lusts and appetites, and not reverently, advisedly, soberly, and in the fear of God; without duly considering either the ends, or the duty of the marriage state.

Q. What is the third relative duty which comes under this command?

A. The duty of masters and servants.

Q. What is the duty of masters and mistresses towards their servants?

A. 1. To consider themselves as placed in this superior state for the glory of God, and the good of the souls committed to their care.

2. To be an example to those who serve them in all holy conversation and godliness.

3. To maintain the worship, and cultivate the fear of God among all who are under their roof.

4. To be reasonable in their commands.

5. To treat them with gentleness, not a lion in their house, and frantic among their servants.

6. To give them that which is just and equal for their service, and with exact punctuality when due.

7. To instruct them in the knowledge, and encourage them in the practice of whatever is for the benefit of *their souls*; and to provide proper food and nourishment for their bodies, considering themselves that they have a master in heaven, to whom they must account for the trust committed to them, and that there is no respect of persons with him.

Q. What is the duty of servants towards their masters and mistresses?

A. 1. To consider their station as of divine appointment, and therefore to serve in singleness of heart, as unto Christ.

2. To honour and respect their persons, as God's vicegerents in that family.

3. To address them with reverence, and always speak of them with respect.

4. To be obedient to all their lawful commands.

5. To be patient under reproof, never answering again.

6. To be honest; not purloining the smallest trifle, but shewing all good fidelity in every thing committed to their care.

7. To

7. To be industrious; not labouring as eye servants and men pleasers, but as the servants of Christ, doing the will of God from their heart.

8. To be frugal; never making the least waste, careful of their interests, as of their own.

9. To be thankful for all the instruction and kindness they receive.

Lastly. To pray for the divine blessing upon their masters and mistresses, and upon all the business in which they are engaged.

Q. What is the fourth relative duty?

A. Between ministers and people.

Q. Is the ministry a divine institution?

A. It is.

Q. Ought no man to take this honour to himself, unless he be inwardly moved by the Holy Ghost?

A. No, in no wise.

Q. What is the duty of a minister in this view?

A. 1. To consider himself an ambassador for Christ, and to feel the weight of that employment.

2. To preach the word of God with all *plainness*, suited to the capacities of the hearers — with *faithfulness*, not afraid of the faces of men — with *diligence*, in season and out of season — with all *wisdom*, rightly dividing the word of truth, that he may give to every man his portion in due season.

3. To give themselves wholly up to the service, unencumbered, as may be, from worldly avocations.

4. To bear meekly the opposition of men of perverse minds.

5. To endure perseveringly, not discouraged by difficulties, or the little success they may meet with.

6. To be the example of the flock, and to have their practice conformed to their preaching.

7. To be often at a throne of grace for the divine benediction upon their labours, that they may not be in vain in the Lord.

Q. What is the duty of the people?

A. 1. To reverence and highly esteem their ministers for their work and their master's sake.

2. To receive with meekness the engrafted word, and diligently attend the ministration of it.

3. To support them with a proper provision of temporal things, the labourer being worthy of his hire.

4. To be followers of them as they are of Christ.

5. To further their success with their utmost countenance and influence.

6. To pray for them, that they may be enabled to be faithful, and for the abundant success of their labours in the conversion of men's souls.

Q. What

Q. What is the fifth relative duty?

A. Between magistrates and subjects.

Q. What is the duty of magistrates?

A. 1. To remember by whose authority they are appointed, and that they are answerable to the King of Kings

2. To exert the power with which they are invested for the glory of God, and the good of their subjects, being a terror to evil doers, and giving praise to them that do well.

3. To consider their offices not as a private emolument, but a public trust, and therefore labouring conscientiously for the public benefit.

Q. What is the duty of the subjects towards their magistrates?

A. 1. To honour them as God's ministers in their several offices.

2. To submit to their just commands, not merely from fear of wrath, but for conscience sake.

3. To avoid carefully all rash censures on them or their proceedings; which may render their persons contemptible, or their authority despised.

4. To contribute to the necessary expences of government; duly paying tribute and custom.

5. To pray for them, that they may be endued with such wisdom and integrity, that under their government, we may lead a quiet and peaceable life, in all godliness and honesty.

Q. What is the fixth relative duty?

A. Between the more elevated in rank and fortune, and the lower ftations in life.

Q. What is the duty of the more elevated in rank or fortune.

A. 1. To confider themfelves under God, as entrufted with many talents, for which they muft give an account.

2. To be condefcending and kind to their inferiors, not treating them as a different race of beings.

3. To affift them with their purfe and influence when oppreffed or indigent.

Q. What is the duty of the lower ranks in life to their fuperiors?

A. To refpect the order of God in the diftinction he hath made,—to pay honour to whom honour is due,—to addrefs them with fubmiffion,—to give them the place of pre-eminence,—not to envy them their fuperiority,—nor be difcontented with their own lot.

Q. What is the laft relative duty?

A. Between the aged, and younger perfons.

Q. What is the duty of the aged?

A. 1. To be examples to the younger, of gravity, fobriety, meeknefs, deadnefs to the world, and heavenly mindednefs.

2. To

2. To advise them from their own long experience.

3. To rebuke the careless and encourage the deserving.

Q. What is the duty of young persons?

A. 1. To honour the face of an old man.

2. To observe a respectful silence before them. Swift to hear, slow to speak.

3. Never to mock their infirmities.

C. These are indeed our duties: and vast the extent of them. The most superficial review of the past, must convince every thinking mind, how often and in how many things we have offended; and whilst we are called to use greater diligence in future, we cannot but feel the vast propriety with which our church puts this humbling cry into our lips after this commandment is read, " Lord have " mercy upon us." 'Tis well for us that we have an advocate with the Father, Jesus Christ the righteous, who is the propitiation for our sins; and that with regard to justification of life, we are not under the law, but under grace.

XXXI.

Q. What is the sixth commandment?

A. Thou shalt do no murder.

Q. Is the accidental killing another, without malice or design, murder?

A. No.

Q. What constitutes the act of murder?

A. That it be wilful, and of malice aforethought.

Q. Does the commandment extend no farther than the atrocious crime of actual murder?

A. Yes, a great deal further.

Q. What does it forbid?

A. It forbids us to hurt any body by word or deed: to bear no malice or hatred in our heart.

Q. Is all anger and passion murder in the heart?

A. Assuredly. Matt. v. 22.

Q. What think you of quarrels, abusive language, and railing?

A. The Scripture saith they that do such things are in danger of hell fire. Matt. v. 22.

Q. Is it unlawful for us even to envy or be jealous of, another's prosperity?

A. It is.

Q. Do you think any provocation can justify hatred?

A. No, in no wise. He that hateth his brother is a murderer. 1 John iii. 15.

Q. Does this commandment extend to every injury done to his soul as well as his body?

A. It doth.

Q. Are

Q. Are we murderers in God's account, if we lead others into sin by our example, solicitation or countenance?

A. To be sure we are. For thereby we injure and destroy the soul, which is much more precious than the body.

Q. What doth this commandment enjoin?

A. All kindness and regard, in heart, word, and conduct towards our neighbours.

Q. When do we possess true kindness *of heart* towards them?

A. 1. When we feel a cordial complacence in their prosperity, whether spiritual or temporal.

2. When we are disposed to put the most favourable construction on every thing they say or do.

3. When we are forbearing and forgiving under provocations.

4. When we feel a tender compassion for their souls and bodies under any afflictions, sufferings, or trials of either.

Q. How should we express our kindness in *word?*

A. 1. To be courteous, in our speech.

2. To be edifying.

3. To say whatever may be for our neighbour's credit, or advantage, avoiding every expression, of envy, backbiting, slander, resentment, disdain, or
ridicule,

ridicule, and every word that might injure or grieve him.

Q. How must we shew our kindness in our *conduct?*

A. By all civility—acts of friendship—good example—and readiness to assist them in every danger, distress and difficulty.

Q. Are we forbid by this commandment to injure ourselves as well as others?

A. Certainly we are. All wilful injuries done to our own bodies or souls, as they are branches of self-murder, are equally forbidden.

Q. Must the whole world and every person in it, if tried by the purity of this law, be found guilty before God?

A. No doubt they must.

Q. Are you and I therefore constrained by it to confess ourselves *murderers?*

A. We are guilty.

Q. And unless we are pardoned this crime, must we perish?

A. We must.

Q. Is there need, therefore, that when this commandment is read, we should cry, *Lord have mercy upon us?*

A. Yes; great need.

Q. Should not a sense of this keep us very low before God?

A. It

A. It ought.

Q. And should it not make us prize highly our redemption in Christ, whereby we are delivered from the curse of a broken law?

A. It should.

Q. Is there not great need of amendment in the best?

A. Very great.

Q. Must we therefore be daily on our knees for grace to incline our hearts to keep this law?

A. Such is our bounden duty.

C. It is indeed. May the Lord of life and love pour out a spirit of prayer and supplication upon you!

XXXII.

Q. What is the seventh commandment?

A. Thou shalt not commit adultery.

Q. Does the commandment extend farther than the outward act here forbidden?

A. Yes. It extends to every desire and thought of the heart.

Q. Who explains it thus?

A. Our Lord in his sermon on the mount. Matt. v. 28.

Q. What do you understand as forbidden by this commandment?

A. All acts, words, and desires of impurity, and all

all intemperance, sloth, and whatever else naturally leads to these.

Q. Where does the Scripture condemn these *impure actions?*

A. Heb. xiii. 4. Gal. v. 19—21. Rom. i. 24—26.

Q. What Scriptures condemn *impure words?*

A. Eph. v. 3, 4. Col. iii. 8.

Q. Where are *impure desires* condemned?

A. Matt. v. 28. 1 Thess. iv. 3—5.

Q. What do you call intemperance?

A. Gluttony and drunkenness.

Q. Do these inflame, and stir up impure desires?

A. They do. Ezek. xvi. 49, 50. Jer. v. 7, 8.

Q. Are they thus doubly criminal?

A. Yes; both in themselves, and in their consequences.

Q. Is idleness and sloth contrary to the spirit of this commandment?

A. It is.

Q. What else is here forbidden?

A. Loose company—indecent dress—immodest pictures—and lewd books.

Q. What is required by this command?

A. To keep my body in soberness, temperance, and chastity.

C. I hope, through God's grace, you will be enabled so to do. We carry about in these fallen bodies our great snare. Lust is the rock on which

which millions split and perish. To gratify a momentary passion, they madly plunge body and soul into hell. Shortlived are the pleasures of sin, but eternal are the torments that succeed them. Be early therefore on your guard. It is easier here to fly from our enemy, than contend with him: easier to beat down the body and keep it in subjection, than to escape from the pollutions that are in the world, when we have sinfully indulged our appetites and sloth in making provision for the flesh to fulfil the lusts thereof. A child of God, therefore, whether he eats or drinks, desires to do it to the glory of God. He eats with moderation to satisfy, not to pamper appetite; and drinks to quench his thirst, not to inflame it; his sleep degenerates not into indolence; he is not slothful in his calling; and his recreations are temperate and innocent. Happy the man that thus walks. Even in this world he tastes, higher, purer, and more solid enjoyments, thou they who cast the reins on the neck of their passions, and his prospects in the world to come, are full of glory. The holy Jesus having promised, Blessed are the pure in heart for they shall see God.

XXXIII.

Q. What is the eighth commandment?

A. Thou

A. Thou shalt not steal.

Q. What is here forbidden?

A. Injustice of every kind, whether committed by open violence, or secret fraud.

Q. Are there other methods of stealing besides housebreaking, robbing on the highway, and picking pockets?

A. Yes, very many.

Q. Is there much injustice committed in worldly dealings and business?

A. There is.

Q. What think you, in buying and selling may we take advantage of the ignorance or necessity of those we deal with?

A. No, in no wise.

Q. May we not ask for our goods a greater price than we ought or mean to take?

A. Certainly not.

Q. Suppose you take bad money, may you not put it away again?

A. No.

Q. Suppose you bought a horse or any other beast, and found it had faults which would lessen its value, would it be robbery to conceal them, when you sold it?

A. No doubt it would be errant knavery.

Q. What think you of running in people's debt,

without

without a design, or reasonable prospect of being able to pay them?

A. I think it as bad, or worse than robbing their house.

Q. Is it theft to sell by short weight and measures?

A. Assuredly it is.

Q. May you take advantage of the necessitous, to buy from them at an undervalue, or to lend them at an unreasonable interest?

A. No. This were cruel oppression.

Q. May we not make always as good a bargain as possible, buy and hire as cheap, and sell as dear as we can?

A. Worldly men call this wisdom, but God, in the day of judgment, will brand them as thieves and as robbers.

Q. Is it any sin to withhold our taxes if we can, or pay as small a portion of them as possible, or buy uncustomed goods?

A. Yes, to be sure. It is as great a sin to cheat the public as any individual?

Q. May we never conceal from the person what is his due, or pay him as small a portion as we can?

A. The wicked do so, but every such transaction is criminal before God.

Q. Does

Q. Does the world count such things as these stealing?

A. Many, I fear, do not.

Q. Can a man have any pretensions to the character of an honest man who does these things?

A. No more than a highwayman.

Q. Is gaming criminal, where superior skill, gives evident advantage?

A. Certainly it is.

Q. Does the servant or labourer rob their masters, when they are idle, or do their work slovenly?

A. They do.

Q. May not a servant give away, or use little matters in the house, though not allowed to do so?

A. No. This is direct thieving.

Q. May a person spend extravagantly upon their persons, or tables, or equipage, or pleasures, what their family may afterwards need?

A. No. This is robbing their heirs.

Q. Is it equally unjust, covetously to withhold from their family, what is needful, and proper for their rank and station?

A. Certainly it is.

Q. Do we owe any thing to the poor?

A. Yes, our alms and benevolence.

Q. Is it robbery of them, when we withhold the affistance they need, and we can afford and ought to beftow upon them?

A. No doubt it is.

Q. If all this is true, dont you think an honeft man is a rare character?

A. Yea, verily. One perfectly fuch is no where to be found.

Q. What does this commandment enjoin?

A. To be true and juft in all my dealings; to do unto others, as if our circumftances were reverfed, I could with juftice expect they fhould do unto me; and to learn and labour truly to get my own living, and to do my duty in that ftate of life, into which it hath pleafed God to call me.

Q. What muft be done if you are convinced you have been difhoneft?

A. I muft humble my foul before God, and make reftitution to the utmoft of my abilities.

XXXIV.

Q. What is the ninth commandment?

A. Thou fhalt not bear falfe witnefs againft thy neighbour.

C. The fixth guards his life, the feventh his chaftity, the eighth his property, and the ninth his reputation.

Q. The

Q. The crimes of perjury, forgery, and the grosser acts of false witness are evident, does the commandment lay a restraint upon the heart and tongue?

A. It doth.

Q. What is forbidden by it?

A. 1. A censorious, and rash judging temper.

2. The malicious pleasure of hearing others faults.

3. All slander and evil speaking.

4. Lying.

5. Tale bearing.

Q. What does the commandment enjoin?

A. 1. A tender regard for our neighbour's character.

2. Candour in our judgment of him, always leaning to the favourable side.

3. To cast a veil over the faults we cannot but see and condemn, and not blazon them to the world.

4. To vindicate the absent, and discountenance detraction.

5. To speak the truth in simplicity.

Q. May we sin against this commandment even when we speak truth?

A. Yes, greatly; if we make our neighbour's faults the matter of our conversation, without any evident

evident charitable necessity, or desire to glorify God.

Q. What think you of those who affect to be wits, and delight to criticise upon and censure others, exposing their mistakes, follies, or infirmities, for the entertainment of their company?

A. Their spirit is malignant, and their tongues set on fire of hell.

Q. Is not the general conversation of the world chiefly built upon the violation of this command?

A. I am afraid it is.

Q. Is it the less criminal for being common?

A. No certainly, rather the more.

Q. Should we not, therefore, take great heed to our lips, that we offend not with our tongue?

A. It needs constant and jealous watchfulness and restraint.

Q. Are we criminal if we join in the laugh, and countenance the ridicule or slander which we hear?

A. Certainly. If we find it improper to bear any other testimony, our silence and seriousness at least should speak our disapprobation.

Q. Have we not all much guilt, think you, lying upon our consciences in this behalf?

A. Very much indeed.

C. We need therefore to seek mercy under this broken law, as well as the rest, and to fly for refuge

fuge to the Saviour of the miserable and the desperate. Wo were to us, if by our own words we were to be justified or condemned eternally. We must instantly plead guilty, and perish; blessed be God that there is help laid on one mighty to save, and that we have in our Jesus a Redeemer complete and perfect, who did no sin, neither was guile found in his mouth.

XXXV.

Q. What is the tenth commandment?

A. Thou shalt not covet thy neighbour's house, thou shalt not covet thy neighbour's wife, nor his servant, nor his maid, nor his ox, nor his ass, nor any thing that is his.

Q. Did not the other commandments forbid evil desires, as well as evil acts?

A. They did.

Q. Wherein does this commandment differ therefore from them?

A. This condemns the corruption of our nature, and that principle of iniquity, from whence all unholy desires, evil words, and works do proceed.

Q. Does the law require perfect purity of nature, as well as purity of temper and practice?

A. It doth.

Q. And

Q. And is it as much broken by the corruption we brought with us into the world, as by any outward acts of sin?

A. It is.

Q. Does the apostle look upon this as highly criminal?

A. He calls it the sin exceeding sinful.

Q. Are the very risings of evil desire criminal, even when not indulged, consented to, or accomplished?

A. They are.

Q. Is this the fault and corruption of every man's nature?

A. It is.

Q. Is all coveting sinful?

A. No.

Q. May we desire to remove any thing inconvenient to us, or to possess any convenience which our neighbour can without injury part with; provided we make him proper satisfaction, and are content and satisfied if he refuse it us?

A. We may so far desire without evil.

Q. But should we be discontented with his refusal, or continue to covet it, is it then sinful?

A. It is.

Q. Are we then transgressors of the whole law, in nature, temper, and practice?

A. We are wholly condemned by it.

Q. We

Q. We can never, therefore, hope to be juſtified before God, by our obedience to a law, that we have ſo entirely broken?

A. No, ſurely. That would be the height of folly.

Q. Where then is our hope?

A. In Chriſt, who hath redeemed us from the curſe of the law, and by his obedience to death is become the end of the law for righteouſneſs to every one that believeth.

C. Remember this. Chriſt is precious to the periſhing ſinner who feels the ſentence of a broken law lying upon his guilty conſcience, and beholds the great Redeemer reſcuing him from the impending ruin. Then the heart cleaves to him in affection, feels the grateful reſentment that ſprings from a ſenſe of his wondrous grace, and conſtrained thereby is powerfully engaged and inclined in all holy obedience, to love and ſerve a pardoning God.

XXXVI.

C. My good child, know this, that thou art not able to do theſe things of thyſelf, nor to walk in the commandments of God, and to ſerve him, without his ſpecial grace, which thou muſt learn at all times to call for by diligent prayer. Let me hear therefore if thou canſt ſay the Lord's Prayer.

A. Our

A. Our Father, which art in heaven, hallowed be thy name. Thy kingdom come. Thy will be done in earth, as it is in heaven. Give us this day our daily bread. And forgive us our trespasses, as we forgive them that trespass against us. And lead us not into temptation; but deliver us from evil. For thine is the kingdom, and the power, and the glory, for ever and ever. Amen.

C. This is the Lord's Prayer, so called, because our Lord himself dictated the words for our use, and left them as a model or directory, that we should pray in this manner. Without God's special grace we have no power either to believe or obey. From him must come the ability for all that he requires, and he hath promised to give his holy Spirit to those that ask him. Whosoever, therefore, careless and profane, lives without prayer, renounces all the baptismal engagements, and manifests a contempt of that grace which alone bringeth salvation. Not that repeating the Lord's Prayer or any other form of words, is praying, if the heart be not engaged. Many teach children their prayers, without teaching them to pray, and many from children get a habit and form of saying their prayers at night, and sometimes in the morning, who do it without any spiritual understanding or real profit to their souls; it will be necessary, therefore,

therefore, before we enter upon the Lord's Prayer, that you should understand the nature of prayer in general, its use, and design, that so you may pray with the spirit, and pray with the understanding also. Tell me then, to whom must prayer be addressed?

A. To God through Christ.

Q. Is it idolatry to direct our prayers to any other being besides the most high God?

A. It is.

Q. Can saints or angels, or any creature, hear and help us?

A. No. In no wise.

Q. May we use their mediation or intercession?

A. No. There is but one Mediator between God and man, the man Christ Jesus.

Q. Is this one of the horrid errors of popery?

A. It is.

Q. Are there different kinds of prayer?

A. Yes.

Q. What are they?

A. 1. Private prayer.

2. Social prayer in our families, and among the faithful.

3. Public prayer in the great congregation.

Q. Can a man pray without speaking?

A. Yes. In his heart.

Q. Does

Q. Does God hear a secret ejaculation, and the groanings and desires that never were uttered?

A. Yes, certainly.

Q. Are these often the most fervent and acceptable prayers?

A. They are, breathing the purest language of the soul.

Q. Is there any real prayer unless the heart be engaged?

A. No. Words without sensibility, are but empty sounds, and useless form.

Q. What is essential then to the nature of true prayer?

A. A heartfelt sense of want stirring up desire of relief, and faith in the promise of God, that in Christ, he will hear and help us.

Q. Can there be no acceptable prayer without these?

A. Certainly not.

Q. Will reading the best prayer that ever was composed, signify any thing, if you do not feel the wants there expressed, and believe the promises there pleaded for?

A. To be sure, it can signify nothing. It is hypocrisy, not prayer.

Q. How often should we pray?

A. Always, when we feel our hearts disposed, and our wants call for relief.

Q. Are there every day particular times that ſtatedly call for prayer?

A. Yes. In the morning when we riſe, to beg God's bleſſing on the day, and at evening when we lye down, to commend ourſelves to his care, and thank him for his mercies.

Q. Is it proper through the day to pray?

A. Yes. At any time when we have leiſure, and particular deſire for ſuch ſecret communion with God.

Q. Should the maſters and miſtreſſes of families daily call their houſeholds together at the throne of grace?

A. It is moſt commendable, and Chriſtian-like ſo to do.

Q. Do you think, that our Lord's injunctions that men ſhould always pray and not faint, are much regarded?

A. I am afraid they are not.

C. Indeed, I fear, but very little. How few live habitually in the exerciſe of private prayer! The moſt riſing up and lying down, as forgetful of God as the beaſts that periſh. How few families call upon the name of the Lord! Where in ſome places through a town, through a village, ſhall we find ſuch a thing as the word of God daily read, and the family called together for God's worſhip! And if with a few the prejudices of education

education are not worn quite off, and the prayers taught them when children, are formally repeated, how careless is the manner, perhaps in bed, or half asleep, without any serious impression of the importance of the subject. I hope you, my dear children, will be particularly attentive to a matter which I so often inculcate: fully persuaded, that till sinners are brought to their knees, and led to seek mercy and strength at a throne of grace, all our labours are fruitless, and our teaching in vain. They who live prayerless must die hopeless, and cannot expect the favour and blessing of God, which they would not even be at the pains to seek.

XXXVII.

C. I informed you the last time we met concerning the nature of prayer in general; we come now to the *Lord's Prayer* in particular, which consists of three parts, the invocation, the petitions, and the doxology, or ascription of praise and glory to God.

Q. Whom are you taught to invoke or call upon in this prayer of our Lord?

A. Our Father which is in heaven.

Q. Is God your Father?

A. He is.

Q. Was you his child by nature?

A. No.

A. No. I was born a child of wrath.

Q. How then come you to be now God's child?

A. Through faith in Jesus Christ.

Q. If God is your Father, is this an encouragement to pray to him?

A. It is.

Q. If you are a child, ought you to have the spirit of a child, confidence, love, and filial fear?

A. I ought.

Q. Does God give this to his children?

A. He doth. Gal. iv. 6. Because we are sons, God hath sent forth the Spirit of his Son into our hearts, whereby we cry, Abba, Father.

Q. Why do you call him *Our* Father?

A. In token of my communion in spirit and prayer with all the children of God in every place.

Q. Are you bound therefore by your prayers to love them as brethren?

A. Assuredly, or else my practice would contradict my prayers.

Q. Doth God fill heaven and earth with his presence?

A. He doth.

Q. Why do you then address him as in heaven?

A. Because there he fixes his throne, and makes the most transcendent manifestations of his presence and glory.

Q. If

Q. If God is in heaven, and we worms and dust of the earth, how should we approach him?

A. With reverence and godly fear, under the deepest sense of our vileness and his Majesty.

XXXVIII.

Q. What is the first petition of the Lord's Prayer?

A. Hallowed be thy name.

Q. What do you understand by the *name* of God?

A. Himself, as manifested to us in all his divine perfections.

Q. What do you mean by the word *hallowed?*

A. I mean that God may be glorified in us and by us, and that the honour due unto his name may be rendered to him by me and all his reasonable creatures.

Q. How are we to hallow God's name as *holy?*

A. By a hearty approbation of all his revealed will, and a humbling sense of my sinfulness.

Q. How must you hallow God's name as *merciful?*

A. By trusting on his mercy, as declared in Jesus Christ.

Q. How are we to hallow God's name, as *almighty,* infinite in *wisdom, faithfulness* and *truth?*

A. I am called to fear his displeasure as the greatest evil—to resign myself to all his dispensations—and to depend upon the certainty of his promises.

C. Thus, in all his perfections, God is to be glorified, and his name hallowed; our hearts, our lips, our lives, should abidingly correspond with, and be under the influence of our prayers. But for this we need God's grace, who alone can enable his people to render him any acceptable service.

Q. Must you, before you can speak this petition, truly feel the want of God's grace, sensible how short you come of his glory?

A. I must, or else I speak without meaning.

C. Observe, therefore, before you pray, the real sensations of your heart, that your worship may be sincere, and your prayers the real language of your soul, not the vanity of words, or the sacrifice of fools, who know not that they do evil.

XXXIX.

Q. What is the second petition in the Lord's Prayer?

A. Thy kingdom come.

Q. What kingdom do you pray for in this petition?

A. The

A. The kingdom of God's grace upon earth, and of his glory which we are expecting in heaven.

Q. What do you mean by *coming?*

A. That it may be set up in my own heart, and in all the elect people of God.

Q. Whose subject was you born?

A. The servant of sin and satan.

Q. How is your state to be changed?

A. By God's grace, who delivers his people from the kingdom of darkness, and translates them into the kingdom of his dear Son.

Q. Are you to beg this blessing from him in prayer?

A. Yes. He hath promised his holy Spirit to those that ask him.

Q. If you pray that the kingdom of grace may be established in your hearts, should you condemn and lament whatever in your temper and conduct is contrary to God's glory, and dishonourable to you as his subject?

A. I ought to do so indeed, and seek to be more faithful.

Q. Would you not otherwise be condemned by your own prayers?

A. To be sure, I should.

Q. Do you desire that God's kingdom may be widely spread through the world?

A. I do.

Q. In

Q. In order to this, what do you here pray for?

A. That God would raise up faithful ministers, preaching with fervency and zeal the gospel of the kingdom, and that he would make their labours abundantly effectual to the conversion, edification, and comfort of his people throughout the world.

Q. Does all the blessing and success of the ministers come from the power of God, in answer to the prayers of his people?

A. It doth, and without this Paul might plant, and Apollos water in vain.

Q. Do you also in this prayer desire that God's kingdom of glory everlasting may come?

A. I do.

Q. Is it then the desire of every faithful soul to depart and be with Christ?

A. It is.

Q. Will not your heart and affections therefore be in heaven now, if your prayers are sincere?

A. Certainly they will.

Q. Suppose God was to answer immediately this prayer, and hasten his kingdom, would it not be terrible to many who are repeating this petition?

A. I am afraid it would.

Q. Does not this prove the hypocrisy of those who pray, for that, which, so far from desiring as a mercy, they dread as the greatest evil?

A. No

A. No doubt it does.

C. Alas! how many more repeat this prayer in hypocrisy, than in sincerity? How little are these awful words pondered before they are uttered! How few think what they are asking, and how startled would they be to have God instantly declare the grant of their request; to hear the archangel's trumpet, to behold a dissolving world, and to meet the Judge of all coming in the clouds of heaven, to take the kingdom for his own! Yet is all this implied in the meaning of thy kingdom come, and none can take it safely in their lips, who have not some good hope through grace, and who cannot from their hearts join the Bride and Spirit in crying, Come Lord Jesus, come quickly, even so. Amen.

XL.

Q. What is the third petition of the Lord's Prayer?

A. Thy will be done on earth as it is in heaven.

C. God's name is truly hallowed, and his kingdom then established in the earth, when this is really the case.

Q. How is the will of God made known to us?

A. By his precepts, and by his providences.

Q. Where

Q. Where are you to learn the *preceptive* will of God?

A. In his revealed word.

Q. Is it from the Bible alone that we know how to walk and to please God?

A. It is.

Q. Should not those who pray for this, therefore, diligently read and meditate upon their Bibles?

A. To be sure, they should.

Q. What think you of those who so often say this prayer, and so seldom examine their Bibles, to know what is the will of God?

A. I think it is impossible they should mean what they say.

Q. How must you perform the will of God so far as it is known to you?

A. As it is done in heaven.

Q. How do the angels in heaven fulfil God's will?

A. In perfection, without defect or delay, and with delight, as constituting their own happiness.

Q. And do you think that you thus do the will of God upon earth?

A. No. I come very short of it, and through the weakness of my nature cannot walk thus upright with God.

Q. Is

Q. Is not this a matter that we should be sorry for?

A. Yes. It is a grief, and cause of humiliation to all the redeemed of the Lord.

Q. But though they do not and cannot attain to this perfection here below, do they approve of it, and long for it, as a thing most desirable?

A. No doubt they do. They could not be God's children otherwise.

Q. Will they ever attain it?

A. Oh yes. I hope so. We shall be shortly like the angels, awaking up in God's perfect likeness, and being for ever satisfied with it.

Q. Will this be the final blessed answer to our prayers?

A. It will.

Q. Do you desire that others should do God's will as well as you?

A. I would that all his reasonable creatures upon earth served him thus in their several vocations and callings.

Q. Does charity, therefore, teach you to make prayers and supplications for all men?

A. It doth.

Q. And do your prayers oblige you to set an edifying example in all holy conversation and godliness before those for whom you pray?

A. They

A. They do: or I should be condemned by my own prayers.

Q. Is God's *providential,* as well as his *preceptive* will to be obeyed?

A. It is.

Q. Does every thing that happens to us come by divine direction?

A. It doth.

Q. May we never murmur or fret under the heaviest afflictions, or severest disappointments?

A. We may not.

Q. Why?

A. Because it is the Lord's doing.

Q. And doth he always what is righteous, just and good?

A. He cannot do otherwise.

Q. What is all impatience, therefore, under our crosses?

A. Rebellion against God.

Q. And is not our folly as great as our sin when we repine?

A. It is, for we quarrel with the dispensations of him, whose goodness and wisdom is infinite.

Q. Yet this folly and sin do we not frequently fall into?

A. We do to our shame.

Q. What effect should that have upon us?

A. It

A. It should teach us more of the vileness of our fallen nature, and stir us up to more importunity and diligence in prayer for grace to help in every time of need.

C. I pray God it may have this effect upon us. Our very failings will then do us good in the issue, when they lay us thus lower in our own eyes, and drive us nearer to God in the spirit of prayer and supplications; and he who is able to keep us from falling, and to restore us when our footsteps slip, hath promised to hear our cry and to help us. Would to God that we were but as ready to pray as he to hear, and as diligent to ask, as he is in Christ Jesus willing to give, not only more than we deserve, but even more than we can desire.

XLI.

Q. What is the fourth petition of the Lord's Prayer?

A. Give us this day our daily bread.

Q. What do you mean by bread?

A. Every thing needful for bodily sustenance.

Q. Does every creature depend upon God for his provision?

A. All are fed by his bounty, and depend on his providence.

Q. Cannot

Q. Cannot all the power and wisdom of man produce a single grain of corn or blade of grass?

A. No. It is God alone who bringeth food out of the earth. Psal. civ. 14, 15.

Q. Do we deserve the least morsel we put in our mouths?

A. No. We have by sin forfeited all God's mercies.

Q. How are they restored to us?

A. In Christ, he giveth us all things richly to enjoy.

Q. Are we to profess our daily dependence upon God in Christ as our Father, who feeds his children?

A. That is our bounden duty.

Q. And is it not our highest privilege that we have a Father to go to, who is able and willing to supply all our wants?

A. No doubt it is.

Q. How often must you ask of God to feed and nourish you?

A. Every day.

Q. How much may you ask?

A. Only the bread of the day.

Q. If God gives you bread to-day, are you to trust on him for the morrow?

A. I am.

Q. Doth

Q. Doth this dependence on God's providence make our care and labour unneceffary?

A. No, in no wife. We muft ufe all appointed means, and depend on him for the bleffing, and fuccefs.

Q. Suppofe a poor man fhould fay, I will pray, and wont work, would that be trufting God?

A. No. It would be tempting, not trufting him.

Q. Are we to be thankful if God hears our prayers, and give us bread to eat, and raiment to put on?

A. Yes.

Q. What? if the bread be coarfe and fcanty, and the raiment poor and thin?

A. Yes. We have no claim for any mercy; all he gives is more than we could demand, and therefore calls for our thanks. Beggars muft not be chufers.

Q. Muft we break our bread to the hungry, trufting upon a frefh fupply?

A. Yes. Though we may not be profufe, we muft not be niggards.

Q. Do we pray for others as well as ourfelves?

A. Certainly.

Q. Can we then with any confcience harden our hearts againft their wants, when we are pretending to pray God to relieve them, and do not give, what he hath put into our hands?

A. The prayers of such are an abomination to the Lord.

XLII.

Q. What is the fifth petition of the Lord's Prayer?

A. Forgive us our trespasses, as we forgive them that trespass against us.

Q. Have we daily cause to pray for the forgiveness of our sins?

A. We have, because we daily offend.

Q. Is it necessary, therefore, that we should have a feeling sense of this, when we pray?

A. No doubt it is.

Q. For whose sake may we hope for the pardon of sin?

A. For Christ's sake only.

Q. Can we never deserve forgiveness for our penitence, or our prayers?

A. No, in no wise.

Q. Have we reason to hope that God for Christ's sake will hear and pardon us?

A. He hath promised to do so.

Q. Must we approach him, therefore, in faith, persuaded of his answering us in mercy?

A. This

A. This is essential to all true prayer.

Q. Can any person be sure that his sins are forgiven?

A. No doubt he may: for this is the privilege of every believer.

Q. Do you think there is no presumption in this confidence?

A. No, certainly. It can never be presumption to believe what God has promised.

Q. But are there not many who are in doubt and fear about their pardon and acceptance, of whom we cannot but hope well?

A. I believe very many.

Q. How comes this about?

A. Through their remaining unbelief, and the weakness of their faith.

Q. May there not be true faith where it is but weak?

A. To be sure there may.

Q. Are our doubts, and fears, and unbelief, to be lamented and condemned?

A. They are, as well as our other sins.

Q. Should every believer desire to attain to higher and fuller assurance in his conscience?

A. This is most desirable, and should be one great end of our prayers.

Q. Can all sins, the greatest, be forgiven?

A. They

A. They can, for the blood of Chrift cleanfeth from all fin.

Q. Hath the greateft criminal as free accefs to the throne of grace, and will he find in Chrift as fure a welcome as the greateft faint?

A. There is no difference. Whofoever cometh to God by Chrift, fhall be in no wife caft out.

Q. Is not this a great encouragement to finners to return to God?

A. Affuredly. The goodnefs of God leadeth us to repentance.

Q. Muft we forgive others as we hope God will forgive us?

A. Yes. A fenfe of his pardoning love will work love in our hearts.

Q. Muft we forgive our greateft enemies?

A. We muft.

Q. Can any offend us fo highly as we have offended God?

A. No. That is impoffible.

Q. Yet we hope to be forgiven, ought we not therefore to forgive?

A. To be fure we ought.

Q. If we bear malice and hatred in our hearts, will our prayers do us any good?

A. No. They muft bring down a curfe inftead of a bleffing.

G. Remember,

C. Remember, therefore, seriously the import of your own prayers, as nothing can have a more powerful influence upon your conscience, to make you patient, forbearing, forgiving; and the blessing will return upon your own heart, however ungrateful returns you may meet with from others. For whilst you are in faith praying for pardon, and walking in brotherly love, you will be enabled to maintain a sweet sense of God's rich grace to your own soul, and know that your sins are forgiven you for Christ's name sake.

XLIII.

Q. What is the last petition in the Lord's Prayer?

A. Lead us not into temptation, but deliver us from evil.

Q. Though God tries his people, doth he never tempt them to commit evil?

A. No. God cannot be tempted with evil, neither tempteth he any man?

Q. What do you mean then by not being led into temptation?

A. That through his good providence temptation to evil may be removed from me, or that I may be supported against it.

Q. If

Q. If you pray to be delivered from temptation, may you wilfully run into it?

A. No. That were to contradict my own prayers.

Q. If you have been hurt before by temptation, may you not venture to try again on the strength of a good resolution?

A. No, in no wise. For I must surely fall.

Q. How must you then hope to escape temptation?

A. By flying from the things, places, and company, where I have received hurt; or if unavoidably led to them, by looking up to God in prayer for strength and support.

Q. From what evil do you desire to be delivered?

A. From all dangers, ghostly or bodily; from all sin and wickedness; from our ghostly enemy, and from everlasting death.

Q. Must we look up to God for his providential protection from all bodily danger?

A. We must, for we are in jeopardy every hour.

Q. But whence come our greatest dangers?

A. From sin, satan, the world, and our own hearts.

Q. Are these most to be feared, and to be made the matter of our prayer?

A. They are.

Q. Whose

Q. Whose work is temptation to evil?

A. The devil's.

Q. How doth he tempt us?

A. By presenting to us such things in the world as are suited to draw forth the corruption of our hearts.

Q. You have great enemies then to struggle with, whence comes your strength for the conflict?

A. From God alone.

Q. Must not those who do not pray, therefore, be led captive by the devil at his will?

A. Assuredly.

Q. If we are left for a moment to ourselves, are we liable to fall into the grossest crimes?

A. We are. The highest saint of God is only kept, whilst he is looking up to God.

Q. Then should not our latest breath be prayer?

A. It should.

C. I pray God you may find it so by your own blessed experience. Ceaseless in your cries at a throne of grace for all the blessings which God in Christ hath promised to bestow, and for deliverance from all the miseries and evils which a fallen sinner hath deserved; that so you may experience God's love in his pardoning grace, and providential keeping, and escaping the bitter pains of eternal death, may come to his presence and kingdom in glory everlasting.

XLIV. *Q.* What

XLIV.

Q. What is the doxology, or afcription of praife to God, which concludes the Lord's Prayer?

A. "For thine is the kingdom, and the power, and the glory, for ever and ever. Amen."

Q. Is God to be the object of our adoration and praife?

A. Yes. This is the honour due unto his name.

Q. Is it matter of comfort to us, as well as glorious to him, to afcribe this praife to him?

A. It is.

Q. What comfort arifes to us from hence?

A. If the kingdoms are his, and all power in him, then we are fure he is able to hear and anfwer, and all things being under his government, he will glorify himfelf in mercy on thofe who call upon him faithfully.

Q. Why do you fay Amen at the end of this prayer?

A. To teftify my faith, that God will do this of his infinite mercy and goodnefs, through Jefus Chrift our Lord, therefore I fay Amen. So be it.

C. You fee now the import and meaning of the Lord's Prayer, which, if ufed as a form, is fhort, full, and weighty: if ufed as a model, will affift

you

you in all your devotions, and suitably close, and sum up your prayers. I shall add no more to what I have said, than seriously to recommend to you the consideration of your own words, the necessity of frequent and importunate prayer, and the blessed effects that will flow from thence, adding this one word of warning to you, that in the day of judgment, many who call themselves Christians, will find among their chiefest crimes what they trusted upon, and performed as their choicest duties: their faithlessness, carelessness, inattention, and formality in their approaches to God, will fill up the measure of their iniquities, and doom them to the portion of hypocrites condemned by their own prayers.

XLV.

C. The appointed means of grace, in the use of which the child of God is enabled to walk before him and please him, are the word of God, prayer, and the sacraments. We come to consider the last of these which concludes the Church Catechism. Tell me, therefore, how many sacraments hath Christ ordained in his church?

A. Two only, as generally necessary to salvation, that is to say, baptism, and the supper of the Lord.

Q. Though they are *generally* necessary, may not some be saved without them?

A. It is possible that some may die in the faith, who may be so circumstanced as to be debarred of the use of the sacraments.

Q. " What meanest thou by this word sacrament?"

A. " I mean an outward and visible sign of an
" inward and spiritual grace, given unto us; or-
" dained by Christ himself, as a means whereby
" we receive the same, and a pledge to assure us
" thereof."

Q. Is the outward and visible sign of any efficacy, unless attended with the inward and spiritual grace?

A. No.

Q. Do not many content themselves with the shadow instead of the substance, and if they have had water poured upon them, and eat at the Lord's table, conclude themselves Christians; holding the form whilst they deny the power of godliness?

A. I am afraid they do.

Q. What is the outward visible sign or form in baptism?

A. " Water, wherein the person is baptized in the name of the Father, and of the Son, and of the Holy Ghost."

Q. What is the inward and spiritual grace?

A. A

A. A death unto sin, a new birth unto righteousness, for being by nature born in sin the children of wrath, we are hereby made the children of grace.

Q. It is not therefore the water merely, but the real death unto sin, and new birth unto righteousness, that makes you a child of grace?

A. To be sure.

Q. Do you think an infant may receive this heavenly gift, of a death unto sin, and new birth unto righteousness?

A. I do.

Q. Can any man be saved who is not born again?

A. No, certainly.

Q. But you believe infants may be saved?

A. I have Scripture warrant to believe so.

Q. If they are the elect children of God, and presented as such in his house, ought we to forbid water?

A. No, in no wise.

C. You, my dear children, are too young yet to enter into controversy, or to judge of the unhappy divisions that have entered into the Christian world. Baptism has afforded a handle of great contention, and some specious arguments have disturbed the peace of many a gracious soul, and led them to undergo the form of dipping, as if they

they had not been already baptised. The Anabaptists of our day are, I think, the most dangerous seducers of the faithful from the church of England, and most zealous to draw away disciples after them. I condemn not those who follow the convictions of their conscience, I am persuaded there are many among their teachers who are faithful to the great Master. But good men may err, and I wish to testify my sentiments, and to guard you against their errors. All the waters of the ocean cannot make a child of the devil a child of God. And the Greek word for baptism, as every body knows who is acquainted with it, is used in the New Testament for a partial washing or pouring of water, as well as for total immersion. Though I apprehend, it is not on immersion or sprinkling, that the chief stress of the argument urged by the Anabaptists, lies, but in the necessity of the actual exercise of previous faith and repentance, without which, either, as they suppose, is useless. But as children are incapable of this, therefore they refuse them baptism, and require them if baptised before, to be rebaptised. It appears to me that this argument goes too far. For if none are to be baptised but those who are in the actual exercise of faith, who can judge the heart? How easy is it to copy a confession of faith? and for a hypocrite to gain admission? Of what efficacy then is his immersion?

sion? Should he be afterwards converted and turned to God, is he to be baptised again? if not, why should an infant, more than an adult, be rebaptised? Who can prove that an infant may not be capable of spiritual regeneration? if they can be saved, must they not be regenerate? if regenerate, who can forbid water that those should not be baptised, who have received the Holy Ghost? And how melancholy a prospect does this afford to the Anabaptist parent, if he considers every child dying unbaptised as perishing? The practice of our church I honour, and vindicate? 'tis scripture, 'tis reason. God only knows those that are his. All who profess faith, where nothing appears contrary to such profession, we receive into the outward pale of Christ's church. We are assured of Christ's regard for little children, declared by his benediction, and censure of those who would have kept them from being presented to him; we know their angels do always behold the face of our Father which is in heaven; we see a Hebrew child circumcised the eighth day, and receiving the sign of the righteousness of faith; though we know how few real Israelites were found among the adults: we see the man after God's own heart, consoled on the loss of his beloved infant, that he should go to the child, though the child should not return to him. The consolation could not be that he should lie in the grave with him if they were to be eternally separated, but that they should meet again in the world of the blessed: thése hints and many more arguments which might be urged, but I may not enlarge, evidently show the salvability of infants, and as regenerate persons give them a right to baptism. It is not for us to determine who will finally be saved. It is enough that some infants (I will not say all) may be saved. Our church administers to them the ordinance of baptism only, as they are received into the number of God's faithful and elect children, trusting that he will graciously accept us in the charitable work of bringing them to his holy baptism, every precaution in the most solemn manner being taken, and every engagement of the most solemn kind entered into for their being taught as soon as they shall be able to learn, the meaning and solemn importance of the profession they have made. Adults by themselves, infants by their sureties, make profession of repentance and faith, time must prove who are the elect, and who are the reprobate. An elect child, come to years of maturity, needs no repetition of the outward sign. A reprobate, if he was washed a thousand times, cannot lose his Ethiopian hue.

Q. What is the other sacrament?
A. The supper of the Lord.
Q. Why is it so called?

A. Because

A. Because instituted by our Lord the night he was betrayed.

Q. Why was this ordained?

A. " For the continual remembrance of the " sacrifice of the death of Christ, and of the bene- " fits which we receive thereby."

Q. Was the death of Christ a true sacrifice?

A. It was.

Q. What is the outward sign of the Lord's supper?

A. " Bread and wine, which the Lord hath " commanded to be received."

Q. What is the inward part or thing signified?

A. The body and blood of Christ, which are verily and indeed taken and received by the faithful in the Lord's supper?

Q. Do you suppose that the bread and wine are turned into the human body of Christ?

A. No, in no wise.

Q. Is the bread and wine as much bread and wine after consecration as before?

A. To be sure it is.

Q. How come they then to be verily and indeed the body and blood of Christ to the faithful receiver?

A. They seal to him, all the blessings purchased by the broken body and blood shedding of the Son of God.

Q. What

Q. What are the blessings and benefits whereof we are partakers hereby?

A. " The strengthening and refreshing of our "souls by the body and blood of Christ, as our "bodies are by the bread and wine."

Q. Doth true faith as really bring to the soul refreshment and strength, as bread and wine taken, refreshes the weary body?

A. It doth.

Q. Then we must have experience of this, if it be real, must we not?

A. Assuredly.

Q. Without this experimental refreshment, can this sacrament do us any good?

A. No. We have else, only taken the bread and wine, and not the body and blood of Christ.

Q. Is the Lord's supper a means of strengthening faith?

A. It is. The sight of the symbols of a Saviour's crucified body, tends to fix our faith more firmly upon him.

Q. Is it a pledge of spiritual blessings?

A. It is. God doth therein assure us of his good will towards, and that we are very members incorporate into the body of his dear Son.

Q. What is required of them that come to the Lord's supper?

A. To

A. " To examine themselves, whether they " repent them truly of their former sins, sted- " fastly purposing to lead a new life; have a lively " faith in God's mercy through Christ, with a " thankful remembrance of his death; and be in " charity with all men."

Q. Does a child of God every day live in the exercise of repentance?

A. He doth, as every day contracting fresh guilt upon his conscience.

Q. Must we confidently trust on Christ's blood to pardon; on his grace to support; on his Spirit to comfort us; looking up with joyful hope to the day of his appearing and glory?

A. To be sure. We do thus shew forth the Lord's death, and our comfortable confidence of an interest therein till he come.

Q. Will this engage us to lead a new life?

A. Nothing can be so effectual thereunto, as faith in a crucified Jesus.

Q. Have we cause to exercise great thankfulness at the Lord's table?

A. Oh yes. We can never enough be thankful for this sacrifice, from whence there descend to us such transcendent blessings.

Q. Should we be found in the exercise of love and charity to all men?

A. No

A. No doubt we should. If when enemies we were reconciled to God by his death from whom dare we withhold our love and forgiveness?

Q. Do all who come to the Lord's table receive this strengthening and refreshment to their souls?

A. No.

Q. Why?

A. Because they eat and drink unworthily.

Q. What do you mean by eating and drinking unworthily?

A. I mean, 1. When they complain of the bitter remembrance, and intolerable burden of sin; without any heartfelt sense of that bitterness and burden.

2. When they are strangers to the faith of the operation of God, and never knew any spiritual refreshment and strength from an inward experience of the love of God in their hearts.

3. When, instead of amending their lives, they continue after the Lord's supper as before, in the allowed indulgence of their sins.

4. When they have no heart-felt thankfulness for that amazing manifestation of God's love in the gift of his Son.

5. When they live in malice, hatred, slander, and the like tempers shewing evidently, that they are strangers to the spirit of a loving, dying Jesus.

C. Your

C. Your answers are pertinent, and I would to God, that there were fewer who frequent the Lord's table to whom they were applicable. But it is terrible to reflect! of the many who come to the Lord's supper, how few approach with a true heart in full assurance of faith to take this holy sacrament to their comfort! some (horrible to mention!) come merely to qualify themselves for a worldly employment—some, because it is the custom at the three great festivals—some, because they have read the week's preparation, and made up themselves, by a week's preceding unusual strictness—profaning thus the sacred ordinance—formal visitors, not real votaries—and instead of the heart-felt attachment to Christ, of an awakened sinner, and penitent believer, substituting the cold and unmeaning expressions of a wretched book, that only can teach the lips to lie, without the least sensibility in the soul. Much as I wish your early attendance on the Lord's table, yet more do I desire you seriously to examine yourselves before you presume to eat of that bread, and drink of that cup. For as the benefit is great to the faithful, so is the danger great to the hypocrite and unbeliever, eating and drinking damnation to himself, not discerning the Lord's body. You, my dear children, must be conscious how much pains and care I have taken to inform your understandings, so that you will be without excuse, if you neglect so great a salvation. I pray God that he may send his Holy Ghost into your hearts, and give you to receive the truth in the light and the love of it, that so you may live in the exercise of daily communion with a pardoning God, and thus be habitually ready, and pleased to approach the table of your Lord, happy in the present experience of his dying love, and rejoicing in the prospect of the day of his appearing: thus shewing forth the Lord's death till he come!

F I N I S.

www.ingramcontent.com/pod-product-compliance
Lightning Source LLC
Chambersburg PA
CBHW020828230426
43666CB00007B/1152